Looking Deeply

Looking Deeply

Vivekacūḍāmaṇi of Śrī Śaṅkarācārya

with translation and notes by
Swami Tyagananda

RAMAKRISHNA VEDANTA SOCIETY
BOSTON, USA

CONTENTS

Preface

When I look at a tree, I see the tree. That's kind of obvious. But when I look at the tree carefully, I see a lot more. I notice the shape and color of its leaves, its flowers, its fruits, and I notice the birds and I hear them chirp. When I go closer and look at the tree more deeply, I may even see ants and tiny insects which have made the tree their home. I may be able to gauge the age of the tree and assess whether it is getting the nutrients it needs for healthy growth.

Looking at myself is not any different from looking at a tree. A superficial look reveals only a superficial me—the me I see when I stand before a mirror. When I look at myself carefully, I notice the me who thinks and feels, whose heart is filled with hopes and fears, whose being is nourished by memories of the past and dreams for the future. When I go deeper and look at myself even more carefully, I see what I may have never seen before. I see my own self —the *real* me—hidden under the layers of the body and the mind.

What is the nature of this real me? Why does the real me remain hidden? How is this real me connected with everyone and everything? The book in your hand addresses these questions, and tries to understand the relationship between me and the rest of the world, also between me and whatever or whoever else there may be beyond the world of my perception and imagination.

Understanding, in the truest sense of the term, begins with looking at everything with care and attention. When we look deeply, we see the finer details, the subtler reality, the inner truth. It is then that we can distinguish between what is essential and what is not, what is intrinsic and what is not, who I am and who I am not, what this world is and what this world is not. That is what discernment means —seeing things as they are and then separating the chaff from the grain. The Sanskrit word for discernment is *viveka*.

Discernment is the foremost practice in Vedānta. All other Vedānta practices become meaningful and fruitful only when they are powered by discernment. If discernment were a jewel, it would occupy the most prominent spot on a royal crown. Hence the title of the text, *Vivekacūḍāmaṇi,* which affirms the preeminence of discernment in Vedānta practice. But it may also point to Vedānta itself as "that which has discernment as its crest jewel."

The seminal works of Śrī Śaṅkarācārya (788-820 CE) are his profound commentaries on the three foundational texts (*prasthāna-traya*) of Vedānta: namely, the Upaniṣads, the Bhagavad Gītā, and the *Brahma-Sūtra*. Studying these texts and the commentaries is immensely enriching, but it is also most demanding, requiring of the student a measure of proficiency in grammar (*vyākaraṇa*) as well as in Sāṃkhya, Nyāya and Mīmāṃsa philosophies.

Relatively less demanding, and hence more accessible, is the study of smaller treatises (*prakaraṇa grantha*). These generally focus on specific aspects of Vedānta teaching, presented with clarity and precision, and in a more digestible form. Śrī Śaṅkarācārya wrote many such treatises as well, better known among them are *Ś ataślokī, Sarva-Vedānta-Sāra-Saṅgraha, Upadeśa-Sāhasrī,* and *Vivekacūḍāmaṇi.*

Among all of Śrī Śaṅkarācārya's writings, the *Vivekacūḍāmaṇi* has remained for centuries a favorite of Vedānta students. It follows a systematic scheme in its presentation but, because its 580 verses are not subdivided into chapters or sections (unlike the Bhagavad Gītā, for instance), getting a handle on the text becomes a challenge for many.

For that reason, I have divided the text into four sections. The first section is introductory. It describes the basic disciplines for a student's fitness to study and practice Vedānta. This sets the stage for a dialogue between the student and the teacher. The second section applies discernment to distill the meaning of "this" (world), "that" (the reality beyond), and "me" (the individual). This is done as a preparation for an analysis of the Upaniṣadic teaching: "You are that" (*tat tvam asi*), which is the focus of section three.

All of this is not meant to be merely an intellectual exercise but something to be experienced directly. Everything that we see with the senses and imagine with the mind is the result of misperception. When we look deeply, we see clearly the truth of nonduality. The Ātman, who is the *real* me, is consciousness—birthless and deathless, pure and perfect. The Ātman alone exists. Experiencing oneness with this nondual existence and dwelling in that timeless reality is real freedom.

In the concluding section we then read the exchange between the newly enlightened student and the teacher who is delighted to see the transformation. When the text is studied with diligence and attention, it quickly becomes apparent that the one referred to as the student or disciple (*śiṣya*) in the text is really none other than the reader, and the teacher (*guru*) is Śrī Śaṅkara himself. When that happens, the study becomes personal and the hope of being enlightened becomes real.

The division of *Vivekacūḍāmaṇi* into sections and subsections was inspired by an outline of the text that Prof. Francis X. Clooney, S.J., of Harvard University, generously shared with me a few years ago. My heartfelt gratitude to him for the outline and for his valuable suggestions after reading a draft of this book. I am grateful to Pravrajika Vrajaprana of the Vedānta Society of Southern California in Santa Barbara for her expertise in editing the manuscript.

My first opportunity to study the text came in the 1970s. It was taught by Sri Ganesh Shastri Joshi to the monks of the Ramakrishna Order at the Mumbai Math. In the 1990s I got a chance to study it again in the Chennai Math under the guidance of Sri V. R. Kalyana- sundara Sastrigal. This provided a good foundation to my understanding of Vedānta and its practice.

When my guru, Swami Vireswarananda (1892-1985), blessed me and taught me how to meditate, he made no mention of the Ātman. To my 20-year-old self this seemed odd. Not long after my spiritual initiation (*dīkṣā*), I sought his guidance. I told him, "I always try to think of myself as the Ātman. Is that compatible with my meditation practice?" I still remember the sweet smile that lit up his face as he said to me, "That is what everyone should do all the time!" Perhaps thinking that I might venture on some innovations of my own, he gently added, "While doing *japa* (repetition of the mantra) and meditation, simply follow the instructions that I gave you."

My guru gave me everything I needed in spiritual life, most of all his assurance regarding the Ātman. With my heart filled with love, reverence and gratitude, I dedicate to him this book which looks deeply at the core of our existence and discovers the Ātman—the pure, perfect and infinite being that you and me and everyone else is.

✳

1

PROLOGUE

Like most traditional Vedānta texts, the book begins with a salutation (*maṅgalācaraṇa*) and, after a few introductory verses, discusses the four basic disciplines (*sādhana-catuṣṭaya*) and initiates a dialogue between the disciple (*śiṣya*) and the teacher (*guru*).

सर्ववेदान्तसिद्धान्तगोचरं तमगोचरम् ।

गोविन्दं परमानन्दं सद्गुरुं प्रणतोऽस्म्यहम् ॥ १

I bow down to Govinda, who is supremely blissful, who is a true teacher, whose nature is beyond the reach (of the mind and the senses) but can be known from the conclusive truth reached in Vedānta. (1)

It is customary to begin a new project with salutation to God and to one's teacher. In this verse, "Govinda" refers to Śrī Śaṅkarācārya's teacher Śrī Govindapāda and, simultaneously, also to God, since the literal meaning of Govinda is "revealer (or protector) of the Vedas."

जन्तूनां नरजन्म दुर्लभमतः पुंस्त्वं ततो विप्रता

तस्माद्वैदिकधर्ममार्गपरता विद्वत्त्वमस्मात्परम् ।

आत्मानात्मविवेचनं स्वनुभवो ब्रह्मात्मना संस्थितिः

मुक्तिर्नो शतजन्मकोटिसुकृतैः पुण्यैर्विना लभ्यते ॥ २

It is rare for beings to obtain a human birth. Progressively even more rare to obtain are a male body, a brahmin birth, steadfast dedication to the Vedic religious path, scholarship, the ability to discern between the self and the non-self, the direct experience (of the self), immersion in Brahman as the self, and spiritual freedom—none of these can be had without the merits acquired in millions of births. (2)

> While the advantage of getting a human birth is generally noncontroversial among human beings (we don't know what the animals think of us), the two subsequent "advantages" may raise eyebrows. This verse, along with #4 and 5, reflects—but, importantly, does *not* endorse—the social conditions prevailing more than twelve centuries ago, which privileged males (still largely true) and brahmins (not so much today) over others. Both gender and caste belong to the body. A key teaching in this text is that the body is a product of ignorance. Gender as well as caste are merely markers of social classification, not of a person's true identity. See, for instance, #177, 254 and 377.

दुर्लभं त्रयमेवैतद्देवानुग्रहहेतुकम् ।
मनुष्यत्वं मुमुक्षुत्वं महापुरुषसंश्रय: ॥ ३

The following three are rare and are acquired only through God's grace: (1) a human birth, (2) an intense desire to be free, and (3) the guidance of a great soul. (3)

लब्ध्वा कथंचिन्नरजन्म दुर्लभं
तत्रापि पुंस्त्वं श्रुतिपारदर्शनम् ।
यस्त्वाममुक्तौ न यतेत मूढधी:
स ह्यात्महा स्वं विनिहन्त्यसद्ग्रहात् ॥ ४

If a man does not strive for the freedom of the self after acquiring a rare human birth as well as a male body and mastery of the Vedas, he is a fool who commits "suicide," since it is like killing oneself by clinging to unreal things. (4)

> This verse and the next again refer to the seeming advantage of a "male body," probably because all of this text's readers in the 8th century CE were almost certainly male and had more social privileges. If Śrī Śaṅkarācārya were to compose this text today for a global audience, he would no doubt find a different way to inspire his readers.

इत: को न्वस्ति मूढात्मा यस्तु स्वार्थे प्रमाद्यति ।
दुर्लभं मानुषं देहं प्राप्य तत्रापि पौरुषम् ॥ ५

Is there any greater fool than the man who, having acquired a rare human birth in a male body, neglects his own interests? (5)

> It is lack of discernment (*viveka*) that leads people to chase goals that appear attractive but are *not* in their interests.

पठन्तु शास्त्राणि यजन्तु देवान्
कुर्वन्तु कर्माणि भजन्तु देवता: ।
आत्मैक्यबोधेन विना विमुक्ति:
न सिध्यति ब्रह्मशतान्तरेपि ॥ ६

People may study scriptures, sacrifice to the gods, do work, and worship the deities but, without experiencing oneness with Ātman, spiritual freedom cannot be achieved even in a span that equals hundreds of Brahmā's lifetimes. (6)

"Work" generally implies religious rituals authorized by the Vedas (*vaidika karma*), but usually also includes secular activity (*laukika karma*).

Brahmā is the aspect of the Personal God who projects the material universe. According to one reckoning, a day in Brahmā's life is equivalent to 432 million human years.

अमृतत्वस्य नाशास्ति वित्तेनेत्येव हि श्रुति: ।

ब्रवीति कर्मणो मुक्तेरहेतुत्वं स्फुटं यत: ॥ ७

According to the Vedas, immortality cannot be attained with the help of wealth. Hence it is clear that work cannot lead to spiritual freedom. (7)

The reference is to Bṛhadāraṇyaka Upaniṣad (2.4.2): "Neither by work, nor by progeny, nor by wealth, but by renunciation alone did some attain immortality."

अतो विमुक्त्यै प्रयतेत विद्वान्

संन्यस्तबाह्यार्थसुखस्पृह: सन् ।

सन्तं महान्तं समुपेत्य देशिकं

तेनोपदिष्टार्थ-समाहितात्मा ॥ ८

Therefore the wise should strive to attain spiritual freedom after giving up the desire for enjoyment of external objects. Approaching an enlightened and virtuous teacher, the mind should be focused on the truth taught by the teacher. (8)

उद्धरेदात्मनात्मानं मग्नं संसारवारिधौ ।

योगारूढत्वमासाद्य सम्यग्दर्शननिष्ठया ॥ ९

After attaining proficiency in yoga, lift the self which is immersed in the ocean of the world, by the self which is dedicated to right perception. (9)

> "Proficiency in yoga" (the state of *yogārūḍha*) is described in the Gītā, 6. 4. The non-discerning part of the mind is immersed in the world. The discerning part is disciplined and has clarity. The latter should extricate the former from the morass.

संन्यस्य सर्वकर्माणि भवबन्धविमुक्तये ।

यत्यतां पण्डितैर्धीरैरात्माभ्यास उपस्थितै: ॥ १०

Those who are learned and wise should renounce all work and strive to remain engaged in the pursuit of the Ātman in order to be freed from the bondage of the world. (10)

> Renouncing "work" means giving up not only the activities fueled by desires but also the ego of being the "doer," the agent of action.

चित्तस्य शुद्धये कर्म न तु वस्तूपलब्धये ।

वस्तुसिद्धिर्विचारेण न किंचित्कर्मकोटिभि: ॥ ११

Work is for the purification of the mind, not for the attainment of the Real. The Real is experienced through deep reflection, never through millions of activities. (11)

> The "Real" (with a capital R) is what is *really* real and different from everything else around us which only *appears* to be real. When the mind is purified through selfless activity, it acquires the clarity necessary for "deep reflection" (*vicāra*).

सम्यग्विचारत: सिद्धा रज्जुतत्त्वावधारणा ।
भ्रान्तोदितमहासर्पभयदु:खविनाशिनी ॥ १२

Knowledge of the real rope, revealed through right reflection,
destroys the suffering caused by the great fear of the snake conjured
through misperception. (12)

> The reference is to the classical example of a coiled rope mistaken
> for a snake in a partially lit room.

अर्थस्य निश्चयो दृष्टो विचारेण हितोक्तित: ।
न स्नानेन न दानेन प्राणायामशतेन वा ॥ १३

The truth is confirmed through reflection on the words of the wise,
and not by bathing (in sacred rivers), nor by charity, nor by
practicing breath control a hundred times. (13)

अधिकारिणमाशास्ते फलसिद्धिर्विशेषत: ।
उपाया देशकालाद्या: सन्त्यस्मिन्सहकारिण: ॥ १४

Success depends essentially on the fitness of the disciple. Other
factors such as place and time are supplementary. (14)

> The qualities necessary for "the fitness of the disciple" are
> described in #16–17.

अतो विचार: कर्तव्यो जिज्ञासोरात्मवस्तुन: ।
समासाद्य दयासिन्धुं गुरुं ब्रह्मविदुत्तमम् ॥ १५

Approaching a compassionate teacher who is the best among the knowers of Brahman, the seeker of knowledge should reflect on the nature of the Ātman. (15)

मेधावी पुरुषो विद्वानुहापोहविचक्षण: ।
अधिकार्यात्मविद्यायामुक्तलक्षणलक्षित: ॥ १६

One who is intelligent, learned and skillful in thinking has the qualities needed to be a fit disciple for the knowledge of the Ātman. (16)

See also #42 for a description of qualities in a fit disciple.

विवेकिनो विरक्तस्य शमादिगुणशालिन: ।
मुमुक्षोरेव हि ब्रह्मजिज्ञासायोग्यता मता ॥ १७

Fitness to pursue the knowledge of Brahman belongs only to one who is discerning and detached, who has qualities such as restraint of the mind, and who longs for freedom. (17)

"Qualities such as restraint of the mind" refers to the "six treasures." See #19. The terms "Ātman" and "Brahman" are used almost interchangeably throughout this text, for they refer to the same reality. When the reality is spoken of in relation to an individual, it is called Ātman; in relation to everyone and everything, the same reality is known as Brahman.

Four Basic Disciplines

The following four basic disciplines (*sādhana-catuṣṭaya*) are required in order to be considered a fit disciple (*adhikārī*) for Vedānta study and practice.

साधनान्यत्र चत्वारि कथितानि मनीषिभि: ।

येषु सत्स्वेव सन्निष्ठा यदभावे न सिध्यति ॥ १८

The wise have spoken of four disciplines, possessing which the pursuit of Brahman succeeds; in the absence of which, it fails. (18)

आदौ नित्यानित्यवस्तुविवेक: परिगण्यते ।

इहामुत्रफलभोगविरागस्तदनन्तरम् ।

शमादिषट्कसम्पत्तिर्मुमुक्षुत्वमिति स्फुटम् ॥ १९

(1) First comes discernment (*viveka*) between the real and the unreal, followed by (2) detachment (*vairāgya*) from pleasures here and hereafter, (3) the six-treasures such as restraint of the mind (*śamādi-ṣaṭ-sampatti*), and (4) longing for freedom (*mumukṣutva*). (19)

> The "four disciplines" are interlinked, each being the cause of what follows and the effect of what precedes it. The "six treasures" are often referred to in this text by the phrase "restraint of the mind, etc." (*śamādi*).

The four disciplines are described in the following verses, starting with "discernment":

ब्रह्म सत्यं जगन्मिथ्येत्येवंरूपो विनिश्चय: ।

सोऽयं नित्यानित्यवस्तुविवेक: समुदाहृत: ॥ २०

An example of discernment between the real and the unreal is the firm conviction that Brahman is real and the world is an appearance. (20)

> The term "appearance" (*mithyā*) is used to denote anything that is unreal but somehow *appears* to be real, and is distinguished from "unreal" (*asat*), which does not exist even as an appearance. This is a distinction without difference, for both the terms refer to entities that are unreal.

What is detachment?

तद्वैराग्यं जुगुप्सा या दर्शनश्रवणादिभिः ।
देहादिब्रह्मपर्यन्ते ह्यनित्ये भोगवस्तुनि ॥ २१

Detachment is aversion to seeing and hearing etc. of the ephemeral objects of enjoyment ranging from one's own body to the celestial world of Brahmā. (21)

> By "seeing and hearing etc." is meant activities associated with the five senses of knowledge: seeing, hearing, smelling, tasting, and touching. The "celestial world of Brahmā" (*brahma-loka*) is considered the highest among the heavenly worlds.

The "six treasures" are now described one by one:

विरज्य विषयव्राताद्दोषदृष्ट्या मुहुर्मुहुः ।
स्वलक्ष्ये नियतावस्था मनसः शम उच्यते ॥ २२

Restraining the mind (*śama*) means dwelling steadily on one's goal after repeated detachment from the multitude of sense objects by observing their defects. (22)

विषयेभ्य: परावर्त्य स्थापनं स्वस्वगोलके ।

उभयेषामिन्द्रियाणां स दम: परिकीर्तितः ।

बाह्यानालम्बनं वृत्तेरेषोपरतिरुत्तमा ॥ २३

Restraining the senses (*dama*) means withdrawing both the types of senses from their objects and returning them back to their respective abodes. The best state of withdrawal (*uparati*) occurs when a thought-wave of the mind is without any external support. (23)

> The senses of knowledge (*jñānendriya*) and of action (*karmendriya*) are referred to as "both the types of senses." A thought-wave (*vṛtti*) is a form the mind takes when it comes in contact with external objects, the way water takes the form of the container it occupies.

सहनं सर्वदु:खानामप्रतीकारपूर्वकम् ।

चिन्ताविलापरहितं सा तितिक्षा निगद्यते ॥ २४

Bearing all suffering without resistance, anxiety and grumbling is called forbearance (*titikṣā*). (24)

शास्त्रस्य गुरुवाक्यस्य सत्यबुद्ध्यवधारणम् ।

सा श्रद्धा कथिता सद्भिर्यया वस्तूपलभ्यते ॥ २५

The wise say that faith (*śraddhā*), by means of which the Real is attained, means accepting as authentic the words of the scripture and of one's teacher. (25)

> The acceptance is not expected to be blind; questions are always encouraged (as we will see in this text). Without faith in the authenticity of the teachings of the scripture and the guru, a wholehearted practice is not possible.

सम्यगास्थापनं बुद्धे: शुद्धे ब्रह्मणि सर्वदा ।

तत्समाधानमित्युक्तं न तु चित्तस्य लालनम् ॥ २६

Contentment (*samādhāna*) does not mean pampering the mind but directing it fully toward the pure Brahman. (26)

> To seek only intellectual or emotional satisfaction would mean "pampering the mind." The qualifier "pure" denotes that Brahman is unique and nondual, uncontaminated by the existence of anything else.

The last of the "four basic disciplines" is now described:

अहंकारादिदेहान्तान् बन्धानज्ञानकल्पितान् ।

स्वस्वरूपावबोधेन मोक्तुमिच्छा मुमुक्षुता ॥ २७

The longing for freedom (*mumukṣutā*) is the desire to be free from the bondage of ignorance—meaning, the body and the ego etc.—by knowing one's own true nature. (27)

> The phrase "ego etc." is a reference to the "inner instrument" (*antaḥkaraṇa*) with multiple functions variously characterized as the ego (*ahaṁkāra*), the intellect (*buddhi*), the mind (*manas*), the storehouse of mental impressions (*citta*).

मन्दमध्यमरूपापि वैराग्येण शमादिना ।

प्रसादेन गुरो: सेयं प्रवृद्धा सूयते फलम् ॥ २८

The longing for freedom, even if it is mild or moderate, bears fruit when it matures through the grace of the teacher and the practice of detachment and the six treasures. (28)

वैराग्यं च मुमुक्षुत्वं तीव्रं यस्य तु विद्यते ।
तस्मिन्नेवार्थवन्त: स्यु: फलवन्त: शमादय: ॥ २९

The six treasures become meaningful and fruitful only for one whose detachment and longing for freedom are intense. (29)

> Detachment leads to the six treasures which, in turn, lead to the longing for freedom. The presence of the cause (intense detachment) in a person guarantees the authenticity of the effect (six treasures) and makes them "meaningful" (*arthavantaḥ*). The presence of the effect (intense longing for freedom) affirms the value of the cause (six treasures) and reveals it to have been "fruitful" (*phalavantaḥ*).

एतयोर्मन्दता यत्र विरक्तत्वमुमुक्षयो: ।
मरौ सलिलवत्तत्र शमादेर्भानमात्रता ॥ ३०

The six treasures are only a façade—like mirage in a desert—when these two, detachment and longing for freedom, are feeble. (30)

मोक्षकारणसामग्र्यां भक्तिरेव गरीयसी ।
स्वस्वरूपानुसन्धानं भक्तिरित्यभिधीयते ।
स्वात्मतत्त्वानुसंधानं भक्तिरित्यपरे जगु: ॥ ३१

Devotion (*bhakti*) is the greatest among the means to spiritual freedom. Exploration of one's own true nature is called devotion. According to others, devotion is the exploration of the nature of one's self. (31)

> Of the two definitions, the first—exploration of one's own true nature—is known as *nididhyāsana*. The second definition refers to

practices which help to discover the embodied self (*jīva*) and its relation to the supreme self (*paramātman*) or the supreme ruler (*parameśvara*).

The Disciple and the Teacher

उक्तसाधनसंपन्नस्तत्त्वजिज्ञासुरात्मन: ।

उपसीदेद्गुरुं प्राज्ञं यस्माद्बन्धविमोक्षणम् ॥ ३२

Equipped with the practices described above, the disciple seeking the knowledge of the Ātman should take refuge in an enlightened teacher, who can bestow freedom from bondage. (32)

What kind of qualities is a teacher expected to have?

श्रोत्रियोऽवृजिनोऽकामहतो यो ब्रह्मवित्तम: ।

ब्रह्मण्युपरत: शान्तो निरिन्धन इवानल: ।

अहेतुकदयासिन्धुर्बन्धुरानमतां सताम् ॥ ३३

The teacher is one who is an adept in the scriptures, free from vice, unaffected by desire, a profound knower of Brahman, immersed in Brahman, calm like the fire with depleted fuel, an ocean of unconditional compassion, and a friend to those who are good and humble. (33)

The metaphor of "the fire with depleted fuel" is found in the Śvetāśvatara Upaniṣad, 6. 19.

तमाराध्य गुरुं भक्त्या प्रह्मप्रश्रयसेवनै: ।

प्रसन्नं तमनुप्राप्य पृच्छेज्ज्ञातव्यमात्मन: ॥ ३४

Worshiping with devotion, prostration and humble service, the disciple should please the teacher and ask about whatever needs to be known. (34)

The disciple now addresses the teacher:

स्वामिन्नमस्ते नतलोकबन्धो
कारुण्यसिन्धो पतितं भवाब्धौ ।
मामुद्धरात्मीयकटाक्षदृष्ट्या
ऋज्व्यातिकारुण्यसुधाभिवृष्ट्या ॥ ३५

"O Master, I bow down to you, a friend of the lowly and an ocean of compassion. Fallen as I have in the sea of the world, please rescue me by your loving glance which showers the nectar of supreme compassion. (35)

दुर्वारसंसारदवाग्नितप्तं दोधूयमानं दुरदृष्टवातैः ।
भीतं प्रपन्नं परिपाहि मृत्योः शरण्यमन्यद्यदहं न जाने ॥ ३६

"I am being scorched in the uncontrollable forest fire of saṁsāra, which is fed by the winds of my bad karma. Please protect me from death. I don't know anyone else in whom I can take refuge. (36)

The world of appearances, fleeting and continually changing, is known as saṁsāra. It is often compared to the ocean, which is difficult to cross. The word "saṁsāra" appears throughout this text.

शान्तो महान्तो निवसन्ति सन्तो
वसन्तवल्लोकहितं चरन्तः ।

26

तीर्णाः स्वयं भीमभवार्णवं जनान्

अहेतुनान्यानपि तारयन्तः ॥ ३७

"There are calm and noble saints who, like the spring, live for doing good to others. Having themselves crossed the terrible ocean that this world is, they save other people as well without expecting anything in return. (37)

अयं स्वभावः स्वत एव यत्पर-

श्रमापनोदप्रवणं महात्मनाम् ।

सुधांशुरेष स्वयमर्ककर्कश-

प्रभाभितप्तामवति क्षितिं किल ॥ ३८

"Such is the nature of great souls: they spontaneously remove the suffering of others. They are like the moon which cools the earth scorched by the burning heat of the sun. (38)

ब्रह्मानन्दरसानुभूतिकलितैः पूतैः सुशीतैर्युतैः

युष्मद्वाक्कलशोज्झितैः श्रुतिसुखैर्वाक्यामृतैः सेचय ।

सतप्तं भवताप-दावदहन-ज्वालाभिरेनं प्रभो

धन्यास्ते भवदीक्षण-क्षणगतेः पात्रीकृताः स्वीकृताः ॥ ३९

"O Master, scorched as I am by the burning heat of the forest fire of the world, please sprinkle on me the sacred, cooling, pure, and nectar-like soothing words of the Vedas, powered by the experience of the bliss of Brahman, issuing from your lips as from a pitcher. Blessed are those who receive your compassionate look and are accepted by you. (39)

कथं तरेयं भवसिन्धुमेतं
का वा गतिर्मे कतमोऽस्त्युपाय: ।
जाने न किञ्चित्कृपयाऽव मां प्रभो
संसारदु:ख-क्षतिमातनुष्च ॥ ४०

"How do I cross the ocean that this world is? What is in store for me? What should I do?—I have not the slightest idea about this. Please protect me, O Master. Please destroy this sorrow of worldly existence." (40)

तथा वदन्तं शरणागतं स्वं
संसारदावानल-तापतप्तम् ।
निरीक्ष्य कारुण्यरसार्द्र-दृष्ट्या
दद्यादभीतिं सहसा महात्मा ॥ ४१

Looking with eyes filled with compassion at the disciple who is seeking refuge and has spoken thus, the teacher at once instills fearlessness in the disciple who is scorched by the forest fire of the world. (41)

विद्वान् स तस्मा उपसत्तिमीयुषे
मुमुक्षवे साधु यथोक्तकारिणे ।
प्रशान्तचित्ताय शमान्विताय
तत्त्वोपदेशं कृपयैव कुर्यात् ॥ ४२

The wise teacher graciously teaches the highest truth to the disciple, who is good, obedient, peaceful, and self-restrained, and who has approached the teacher in a prescribed manner with a longing for freedom. (42)

With minor variations, this verse is similar to the Muṇḍaka Upaniṣad, 1.2.13. The qualities of a fit disciple are also described in #16-17.

मा भैष्ट विद्वंस्तव नास्त्यपायः
संसारसिन्धोस्तरणेऽस्त्युपायः ।
येनैव याता यतयोऽस्य पारं
तमेव मार्गं तव निर्दिशामि ॥ ४३

"Fear not, O wise one, no harm will come to you. There *is* a way to go beyond the ocean of saṁsāra. I shall show you the path, following which spiritual seekers have crossed the ocean. (43)

अस्त्युपायो महान्कश्चित्संसारभयनाशनः ।
तेन तीर्त्वा भवाम्भोधिं परमानन्दमाप्स्यसि ॥ ४४

"There is a great method which will destroy your fear of saṁsāra. With its help, you will cross the ocean that this world is and attain supreme bliss. (44)

वेदान्तार्थ-विचारेण जायते ज्ञानमुत्तमम् ।
तेनात्यन्तिक-संसारदुःखनाशो भवत्यनु ॥ ४५

"Supreme knowledge is attained through reflection on the words of Vedānta, which totally destroys the suffering caused by saṁsāra. (45)

श्रद्धा-भक्ति-ध्यान-योगान्मुमुक्षो:
मुक्तेहेर्तून्वक्ति साक्षात् श्रुतेर्गी: ।
यो वा एतेष्वेव तिष्ठत्यमुष्य
मोक्षोऽविद्याकल्पिताद्देहबन्धात् ॥ ४६

"The Vedas declare deep faith (*śraddhā*), devotion (*bhakti*) and meditation (*dhyāna*) to be the means to spiritual freedom. One who practices these becomes free from the bondage of the body which is caused by ignorance. (46)

The Vedic reference is to the Kaivalya Upaniṣad, 1. 2.

अज्ञानयोगात्परमात्मनस्तव
ह्यनात्मबन्धस्तत एव संसृति: ।
तयोर्विवेकोदित-बोधवह्नि:
अज्ञानकार्यं प्रदहेत्समूलम् ॥ ४७

"You, the supreme self, are in bondage to non-self because of your ignorance, which has resulted in transmigration. The fire of knowledge produced by discernment between the two—the self and the non-self—destroys the result of ignorance along with its cause." (47)

॥ शिष्य उवाच ॥
कृपया श्रूयतां स्वामिन्प्रश्नोऽयं क्रियते मया ।
यदुत्तरमहं श्रुत्वा कृतार्थ: स्यां भवन्मुखात् ॥ ४८

The disciple said:

O Master, please hear this question of mine. Listening to its answer from your lips I will be fulfilled. (48)

को नाम बन्ध: कथमेष आगत:

कथं प्रतिष्ठास्य कथं विमोक्ष: ।

कोऽसावनात्मा परम: क आत्मा

तयोर्विवेक: कथमेतदुच्यताम् ॥ ४९

Please tell me: What is bondage? How did it arise? How does it exist? How is freedom attained? Who is this non-self? Who is the supreme self? How is discernment practiced between the two? (49)

All of these seven questions asked by the disciple are answered in the rest of the book. See especially #69–70, 72–123, 125–57.

The teacher praises the disciple and appreciates the questions before answering them:

॥ श्रीगुरुरुवाच ॥

धन्योऽसि कृतकृत्योऽसि पावितं ते कुलं त्वया ।

यदविद्याबन्ध-मुक्त्या ब्रह्मीभवितुमिच्छसि ॥ ५०

The teacher said:

Seeking freedom from the bondage of ignorance and being Brahman, you are doing what needs to be done. You are truly blessed and you have honored your family lineage. (50)

ऋणमोचनकर्तार: पितु: सन्ति सुतादय: ।

बन्धमोचनकर्ता तु स्वस्मादन्यो न कश्चन ॥ ५१

The father's debts may be paid off by his children and other family members, but freedom from bondage can be attained by no one but oneself. (51)

मस्तकन्यस्तभारादेर्दुःखमन्यैर्निवार्यते ।
क्षुधादिकृतदुःखं तु विना स्वेन न केनचित् ॥ ५२

The burden of the load on one's head can be shared by others, but one's pangs of hunger etc. are suffered by no one but oneself. (52)

पथ्यमौषधसेवा च क्रियते येन रोगिणा ।
आरोग्यसिद्धिर्दृष्टाऽस्य नान्यानुष्ठितकर्मणा ॥ ५३

Health is restored when diet and medicine are taken by the patient, not when taken by someone else. (53)

वस्तुस्वरूपं स्फुटबोधचक्षुषा
स्वेनैव वेद्यं न तु पण्डितेन ।
चन्द्रस्वरूपं निजचक्षुषैव
ज्ञातव्यमन्यैरवगम्यते किम् ॥ ५४

The true nature of things is revealed through one's own clear awareness, not through a scholar's. The form of the moon is perceived through one's own eyes, not through someone else's. (54)

अविद्या-काम-कर्मादि-पाशबन्धं विमोचितुम् ।
कः शक्नुयाद्विनात्मानं कल्पकोटिशतैरपि ॥ ५५

Who else but me can free myself from the binding noose of ignorance, desire, karma and its results even in a thousand million creation-cycles? (55)

The "binding noose" is a chain reaction that is triggered by ignorance, successively producing desire, karma, and the repeated suffering as "its results."

न योगेन न सांख्येन कर्मणा नो न विद्यया ।

ब्रह्मात्मैकत्व-बोधेन मोक्ष: सिध्यति नान्यथा ॥ ५६

Spiritual freedom is attained through knowing that the Ātman and Brahman are one, not through Yoga or Sāmkhya or work or ritual. (56)

> Our bondage is the result of ignorance (*ajñāna*) regarding the identity of the Ātman and Brahman. It naturally follows that freedom can be reclaimed by eliminating ignorance, which only knowledge (*jñāna* or *bodha*) can do. Everything else can be, at best, only an indirect aid in the effort.

वीणाया रूपसौन्दर्यं तन्त्रीवादनसौष्ठवम् ।

प्रजारञ्जनमात्रं तन्न साम्राज्याय कल्पते ॥ ५७

वाग्वैखरी शब्दझरी शास्त्रव्याख्यान-कौशलम् ।

वैदुष्यं विदुषां तद्वद्-भुक्तये न तु मुक्तये ॥ ५८

The beauty of the vīṇā and the expertise in playing it can only entertain people; these do not lead to an absolute supremacy (over everything). In the same way, expertise in language, fluency in talk, proficiency in interpreting scriptures, and scholarship can only entertain scholars; these do not lead to spiritual freedom. (57-58)

> Vīṇā is an Indian string instrument, which is mentioned in the Vedas. The beauty of the instrument and the expertise in playing it have only a limited utility, like expertise in language, etc.

अविज्ञाते परे तत्त्वे शास्त्राधीतिस्तु निष्फला ।
विज्ञातेऽपि परे तत्त्वे शास्त्राधीतिस्तु निष्फला ॥ ५९

The study of scriptures is useless if the highest truth is not known.
The study of scriptures is useless also if the highest truth *is* known.
(59)

> The study of scriptures without discernment and detachment is
> useless, for it cannot reveal the highest truth. It is equally useless
> after the highest truth *is* known, for the purpose of the study is
> already achieved.

शब्दजालं महारण्यं चित्तभ्रमणकारणम् ।
अत: प्रयत्नाज्ज्ञातव्यं तत्त्वज्ञैस्तत्त्वमात्मन: ॥ ६०

The web of words is a huge forest which causes the mind to wander.
Efforts therefore must be made by the wise to know the nature of
the Ātman. (60)

अज्ञानसर्पदष्टस्य ब्रह्मज्ञानौषधं विना ।
किमु वेदैश्च शास्त्रैश्च किमु मन्त्रै: किमौषधै: ॥ ६१

Without the medicine of the knowledge of Brahman, of what use are
the Vedas, scriptures, mantras, and medicine to a person who is
bitten by the snake of ignorance? (61)

न गच्छति विना पानं व्याधिरौषधशब्दत: ।
विनाऽपरोक्षानुभवं ब्रह्मशब्दैर्न मुच्यते ॥ ६२

Illness is not cured by hearing about medicine but by drinking it. Freedom is not attained by hearing about Brahman but by experiencing it. (62)

अकृत्वा दृश्यविलयमज्ञात्वा तत्त्वमात्मनः ।
ब्रह्मशब्दैः कुतो मुक्तिरुक्तिमात्रफलैर्नृणाम् ॥ ६३

Without sublimating what is perceived and without knowing the true nature of the self, how can people attain spiritual freedom merely by uttering the word "Brahman"? (63)

अकृत्वा शत्रुसंहारमगत्वाखिलभूश्रियम् ।
राजाहमिति शब्दान्नो राजा भवितुमर्हति ॥ ६४

Without conquering the enemies and without gaining enormous wealth, no one becomes a king merely by saying, "I am the king." (64)

आप्तोक्तिं खननं तथोपरिशिलाद्युत्कर्षणं स्वीकृतिं
निक्षेपः समपेक्षते न हि बहिः शब्दैस्तु निर्गच्छति ।
तद्वद्ब्रह्मविदोपदेश-मननध्यानादिभि-र्लभ्यते
मायाकार्य-तिरोहितं स्वममलं तत्त्वं न दुर्युक्तिभिः ॥ ६५

A buried treasure is retrieved not merely by urging it to come out but through expert advice, digging, removing of the overlaying stones etc., and grasping it. In the same way, one's pure nature, which is buried under māyā and its effects, is experienced not with bad reasoning but with practices such as reflection and meditation, after receiving instruction from an enlightened being. (65)

तस्मात्सर्वप्रयत्नेन भवबन्धविमुक्तये ।
स्वैरेव यत्न: कर्तव्यो रोगादाविव पण्डितै: ॥ ६६

The wise should, therefore, make all efforts on their own, as is done during an illness, to be free from the bondage of the world. (66)

यस्त्वयाद्य कृत: प्रश्नो वरीयाञ्छास्त्रविन्मत: ।
सूत्रप्रायो निगूढार्थो ज्ञातव्यश्च मुमुक्षुभि: ॥ ६७

The question you asked today is excellent, the kind that those proficient in scriptures might ask—it is almost like an aphorism (*sūtra*), profound and worthy of being known by seekers of freedom. (67)

शृणुष्वावहितो विद्वन्यन्मया समुदीर्यते ।
तदेतच्छ्रवणात्सद्यो भवबन्धाद्विमोक्ष्यसे ॥ ६८

O wise one, listen attentively to what I explain to you. You will be immediately freed from the bondage of this world by listening to this. (68)

The disciple's question, "How is freedom attained?" (#49), is answered in the following two verses:

मोक्षस्य हेतु: प्रथमो निगद्यते
वैराग्यमत्यन्तमनित्यवस्तुषु ।
तत: शमश्चापि दमस्तितिक्षा
न्यास: प्रसक्ताखिलकर्मणां भृशम् ॥ ६९

I'll first describe what leads to freedom: supreme detachment from all perishable objects, followed by control of the mind and the senses, forbearance, and the immediate giving up of all activities to which one is attached. (69)

These practices were defined in #21-24.

तत: श्रुतिस्तन्मननं सतत्त्व-
ध्यानं चिरं नित्यनिरन्तरं मुने: ।
ततोऽविकल्पं परमेत्य विद्वान्
इहैव निर्वाणसुखं समृच्छति ॥ ७०

This is followed by hearing of the Vedic truths, reflecting on them, and regular and continuous meditation by the seeker. It is then that the wise person experiences the joy of freedom here itself, having reached the supreme which is beyond all duality. (70)

✳

2

"ME" AND "THAT"

All that exists can be described in three simple words: this (*idam*), that (*tat*), and me (*aham*). By "this" is meant the world, everything that is perceived by my senses or imagined by my mind. "That" is the reality, the truth or the being which my mind can imagine as transcending all "this." And "me" is the individual who is doing all the perceiving and the imagining.

When I apply the power of discernment (*viveka*) and look deeply at "this," the world around me, I notice that it changes all the time. The world that I see when I am awake is quite different from the world that I see while dreaming—and the world disappears altogether when I am in deep sleep. Looking deeply, it is possible to see that the world ("this") seems to have no absolute existence and is totally dependent on my perception of it.

When I apply the power of discernment and look deeply at the individual "me," I can see what is intrinsic to me and what is not. Whatever is intrinsic to me is inseparable from my existence. It is my true self, the Ātman. Everything else about me is the non-self.

When I apply the power of discernment and look deeply at "that," the reality beyond, I see a being identified as God (*īśvara*) and there too I discover intrinsic and non-intrinsic elements. That which is intrinsic is the absolute (*Brahman*), the non-intrinsic part is the non-self.

Applying the power of discernment, this section looks deeply at "me" and "that" to find who really I am and who really "that" is.

यद्बोद्धव्यं तवेदानीमात्मानात्मविवेचनम् ।

तदुच्यते मया सम्यक् श्रुत्वात्मन्यवधारय ॥ ७१

I'll now teach you what you need to learn: discernment between the self and the non-self. Listen carefully and ponder this in your mind. (71)

> The self is covered—and hence hidden—by the non-self. Hence the need for discernment between the two. The covering over the self is envisioned in terms of either "three bodies" (*śarīra-traya*) or "five layers" (*pañca-kośa*).

Three Bodies

The Sanskrit word for "body" is *śarīra*, literally, "that which wears out or deteriorates" (*śīryate iti śarīram*). It is possible to think of the Ātman as covered by three bodies—gross (*sthūla*), subtle (*sūkṣma*), and causal (*kāraṇa*)—which "wear out" through discernment. These three bodies constitute the non-self (*anātman*). Their description (#72–123) answers the disciple's question: "Who is this non-self?" (#49)

Now, the description of the gross body:

मज्जास्थिमेद:पलरक्तचर्मत्वगाह्वयैर्धातुभिरेभिरन्वितम् ।

पादोरुवक्षोभुजपृष्ठमस्तकैरङ्गैरुपाङ्गैरुपयुक्तमेतत् ।

अहं ममेति प्रथितं शरीरं मोहास्पदं स्थूलमितीर्यते बुधै: ॥ ७२

According to the wise, the gross body is made of these components: marrow, bones, fat, flesh, blood, skin and cuticle, and consisting of these limbs and their parts: legs, thighs, the chest, arms, the back, and the head. It is viewed as "I" and "mine," and is the cause of delusion. (72)

नभोनभस्वद्दहनाम्बुभूमय:
सूक्ष्माणि भूतानि भवन्ति तानि ॥ ७३
परस्परांशै-र्मिलितानि भूत्वा
स्थूलानि च स्थूलशरीर-हेतव: ।
मात्रास्तदीया विषया भवन्ति
शब्दादय: पञ्च सुखाय भोक्तु: ॥ ७४

Space, air, fire, water and earth are the subtle (*sūkṣma*) elements. Intermixing of these makes them tangible (*sthūla*) and these become the cause of the gross body. The five sense impressions— sound and the rest—become the objects (*viṣaya*) for the experience of the self. (73-74)

The five sense impressions are sound, sight, smell, taste, and touch.

य एषु मूढा विषयेषु बद्धा
रागोरुपाशेन सुदुर्दमेन ।
आयान्ति निर्यान्त्यध ऊर्ध्वमुच्चै:
स्वकर्मदूतेन जवेन नीता: ॥ ७५

Those fools who are tied to these objects with the painful noose of attachment are carried back and forth by their own karma to higher and lower realms. (75)

शब्दादिभि: पञ्चभिरेव पञ्च

पञ्चत्वमापु: स्वगुणेन बद्धा: ।

कुरङ्ग-मातङ्ग-पतङ्ग-मीन-

भृङ्गा नर: पञ्चभिरञ्चित: किम् ॥ ७६

The attraction to even one of these five sense objects, such as sound etc., becomes the cause of death to a deer, an elephant, a moth, a fish, and a bee. What, then, to speak of the human being who is attracted to all of these five! (76)

> Each of the five creatures mentioned in the verse is often lured to its death by the special attraction each has to a specific sensory experience: sound (deer), touch (elephant), light (moth), taste (fish), and smell (bee).

दोषेण तीव्रो विषय: कृष्णसर्पविषादपि ।

विषं निहन्ति भोक्तारं द्रष्टारं चक्षुषाप्ययम् ॥ ७७

A sense object is more poisonous than even the poison of a snake: the poison kills a person only when it is consumed whereas an object can destroy a person when it is merely seen. (77)

> When the mind and the senses go out, the self within is forgotten— and that is tantamount to spiritual "death."

विषयाशामहापाशाद्यो विमुक्त: सुदुस्त्यजात् ।

स एव कल्पते मुक्त्यै नान्य: षट्शास्त्रवेद्यपि ॥ ७८

It is difficult to get out of the powerful noose of desire for sense objects. Only the person who is free from it is fit for spiritual freedom, not anyone else even if they have studied the six schools of philosophy. (78)

The six schools of Indian philosophy (called *darśana*) are Sāṃkhya, Yoga, Nyāya, Vaiśeṣika, Pūrva-Mīmāṃsa, and Uttara-Mīmāṃsa (better known as Vedānta).

आपातवैराग्यवतो मुमुक्षून्
भवाब्धिपारं प्रतियातुमुद्यतान् ।
आशाग्रहो मज्जतेऽन्तराले
निगृह्य कण्ठे विनिवर्त्य वेगात् ॥ ७९

Filled with a frail fit of dispassion and wanting to go beyond the ocean of the world, a spiritual seeker is quickly grasped midway by the neck and drowned by the crocodile of desire. (79)

विषयाख्यग्रहो येन सुविरक्त्यसिना हत: ।
स गच्छति भवाम्भोधे: पारं प्रत्यूहवर्जित: ॥ ८०

One who has killed the crocodile of desire by the sword of genuine dispassion is able to go beyond the ocean of the world without any hurdles. (80)

विषमविषयमार्गे गच्छतोऽनच्छबुद्धे:
प्रतिपदमभियातो मृत्युरप्येष विद्धि ।
हितसुजनगुरूक्त्या गच्छत: स्वस्य युक्त्या
प्रभवति फलसिद्धि: सत्यमित्येव विद्धि ॥ ८१

Know that a person with an impure mind, treading the difficult path of sense objects, is overcome at every step with hurdles, even death. Know this to be true that the destination is reached successfully by one who follows one's reasoning which is trained by the words of the teacher and other holy people. (81)

> The chariot-imagery (*ratha-kalpanā*) in the Kaṭha Upaniṣad (1.3.3-9) describes the sense objects as a path on which the senses (like horses) travel. How the desire for sense objects ultimately ends in one's ruin is described in the Gītā (2. 62–63).

मोक्षस्य कांक्षा यदि वै तवास्ति

त्यजातिदूराद्विषयान्विषं यथा ।

पीयूषवत्तोषदयाक्षमार्जव-

प्रशान्तिदान्तीर्भज नित्यमादरात् ॥ ८२

If you long for spiritual freedom, stay far away from sense objects—as if they were poison—and practice with regularity and sincerity the nectar-like qualities of contentment, compassion, forbearance, simplicity, control of the mind, and control of the senses. (82)

अनुक्षणं यत्परिहृत्य कृत्यं

अनाद्यविद्याकृतबन्धमोक्षणम् ।

देह: परार्थोऽयममुष्य पोषणे

य: सज्जते स स्वमनेन हन्ति ॥ ८३

This body has no inherent value. A person commits suicide by obsessing over its care, instead of not identifying with it and being free from the bondage of beginningless ignorance. (83)

As explained in #4, real suicide is not the destruction of one's body but the neglect of one's true self.

शरीरपोषणार्थी सन् य आत्मानं दिदृक्षति ।
ग्राहं दारुधिया धृत्या नदी तर्तुं स गच्छति ॥ ८४

A person who wishes to see the Ātman while pandering to the needs of the body is like one who wishes to cross a river by holding on to a crocodile and imagining it to be a log of wood. (84)

मोह एव महामृत्युर्मुमुक्षोर्वपुरादिषु ।
मोहो विनिर्जितो येन स मुक्तिपदमर्हति ॥ ८५

To a spiritual seeker, identifying with things like the body is dire death. Only one who has conquered the force of identification is fit for the state of freedom. (85)

> Identification occurs in two primary ways: as "I" (toward body and mind) and "mine" (toward family, friends, home, and other possessions).

मोहं जहि महामृत्युं देहदारसुतादिषु ।
यं जित्वा मुनयो यान्ति तद्विष्णो: परमं पदम् ॥ ८६

Give up the deadly identification with the body, the spouse, the children etc., conquering which spiritual seekers reach the all-pervading supreme being. (86)

त्वङ्-मांस-रुधिर-स्नायु-मेदो-मज्जास्थि-संकुलम् ।
पूर्णं मूत्र-पुरीषाभ्यां स्थूलं निन्द्यमिदं वपु: ॥ ८७

44

This body is disgusting, consisting as it does of the skin, flesh, blood, arteries and veins, fat, marrow and bones, and is filled with urine and feces. (87)

पञ्चीकृतेभ्यो भूतेभ्य: स्थूलेभ्य: पूर्वकर्मणा ।

समुत्पन्नमिदं स्थूलं भोगायनतमात्मन: ।

अवस्था जागरस्तस्य स्थूलार्थानुभवो यत: ॥ ८८

This body is one's receptacle of experience. It is the result of past karma and consists of tangible elements that result from *pañcikaraṇa*. Since the body generates experience of tangible objects, it is identified with the waking state. (88)

Pañcikaraṇa is the process through which the subtle primary elements (*tanmātrā*) become tangible elements (*mahābhūta*).

बाह्यैन्द्रियै: स्थूलपदार्थसेवां

स्रक्-चन्दन-स्त्र्यादि-विचित्ररूपाम् ।

करोति जीव: स्वयमेतदात्मना

तस्मात्प्रशस्तिर्वपुषोऽस्य जागरे ॥ ८९

It is through the body that the individual self experiences diverse tangible objects such as sandalwood and woman with the help of the external senses. The body therefore is vital in the waking state. (89)

"Sandalwood and woman" is a phrase commonly employed in ancient Sanskrit texts to refer to sensual enjoyments—another instance of how in the early centuries it was taken for granted that the presumed reader of the text would invariably be a male.

सर्वो ऽपि बाह्य: संसार: पुरुषस्य यदाश्रय: ।
विद्धि देहमिदं स्थूलं गृहवद्-गृहमेधिन: ॥ ९०

As a home is to a householder, recognize this body to be the tangible abode of a person's experience of the external world. (90)

स्थूलस्य सम्भव-जरामरणानि धर्मा:
स्थौल्यादयो बहुविधा: शिशुताद्यवस्था: ।
वर्णाश्रमादिनियमा बहुधाऽमया: स्यु:
पूजावमानबहुमानमुखा विशेषा: ॥ ९१

The body is subject to birth, aging and death, is prone to shapes like plumpness, has stages like childhood, is bound by rules related to different social classes and life's stages, is susceptible to diverse illnesses, and has experiences like praise, insult and respect. (91)

The subtle body is described in the following verses:

बुद्धीन्द्रियाणि श्रवणं त्वगक्षि
घ्राणं च जिह्वा विषयावबोधनात् ।
वाक्-पाणि-पादा गुदमप्युपस्थं
कर्मेन्द्रियाणि प्रवणानि कर्मसु ॥ ९२

The senses of knowledge—so called because they bring awareness of objects—are ears, skin, eyes, nose, and tongue. The senses of action —so called because they are engaged in activities—are speech, hands, feet, and organs of excretion and procreation. (92)

The "senses" are the subtle counterparts of the tangible organs mentioned above. The sense of hearing, for instance, is not the ear per se, but the *ability* to hear, which is accomplished through the instrumentality of ears.

निगद्यतेऽन्त:करणं मनोधी:
अहंकृतिश्चित्तमिति स्ववृत्तिभि: ।
मनस्तु संकल्पविकल्पनादिभि:
बुद्धि: पदार्थाध्यवसायधर्मत: ॥ ९३

Based on its functions, the inner instrument (*antaḥkaraṇa*) is described as mind (*manas*), intellect (*buddhi*), ego (*ahaṃkāra*), and mind-stuff (*citta*). The mind weighs the pros and cons. The intellect makes decisions. (93)

> Although "mind" is only one of the ways in which the inner instrument can be described, it is also the most popular way by which the inner instrument itself is known.

अत्राभिमानादहमित्यहंकृति: ।
स्वार्थानुसन्धानगुणेन चित्तम् ॥ ९४

The ego produces the awareness of "I" and the mind-stuff stores memory of whatever is meaningful to the person. (94)

प्राणापानव्यानोदानसमाना भवत्यसौ प्राण: ।
स्वयमेव वृत्तिभेदाद्विकृतिभेदात्सुवर्णसलिलमिव ॥ ९५

Although one, the life-force (*prāṇa*) appears as prāṇa, apāna, vyāna, udāna, and samāna, depending on its different functions and modifications, as in the case of gold and water. (95)

Both gold and water retain their essential identity, even as gold can take the form of different ornaments, and water can appear in the form of waves, foam etc. The same is true for *prāṇa* as well.

Prāṇa is only one of the five ways in which life-force manifests, but it is also a popular name for the life-force as a whole.

वागादि पञ्च श्रवणादि पञ्च
प्राणादि पञ्चाभ्रमुखानि पञ्च ।
बुद्ध्याद्यविद्यापि च कामकर्मणी
पुर्यष्टकं सूक्ष्मशरीरमाहुः ॥ ९६

The "city" called the subtle body is made of these 8 constituents: (1) five senses of action, such as speech, (2) five senses of knowledge, such as hearing, (3) five forms of prāṇa, (4) five primal elements, such as space, (5) four forms of the inner instrument, such as the intellect, (6) ignorance, (7) desire, and (8) karma. (96)

The "five primal elements" are space (*ākāśa*), air (*vāyu*), fire (*agni*), water (*ap*), and earth (*pṛthivi*).

इदं शरीरं शृणु सूक्ष्मसंज्ञितं
लिङ्गं त्वपञ्चीकृतभूतसम्भवम् ।
सवासनं कर्मफलानुभावकं
स्वाज्ञानतोऽनादिरुपाधिरात्मनः ।
स्वप्नो भवत्यस्य विभक्त्यवस्था
स्वमात्रशेषेण विभाति यत्र ॥ ९७

Listen to this—known to be subtle, this body is the symbol of the self and is made of the elements before *pañcikaraṇa*. It contains latent mental impressions, and the results of karma are experienced through it. Its superimposition on the Ātman is timeless, resulting from the Ātman's own ignorance. The dream is its distinct state, where it truly shines as itself. (97)

> The functioning of the subtle body is obvious in the dream state, but not so in the waking state because of the presence of the gross body, and not in deep sleep because in it the subtle body itself becomes nonfunctional. In dream the subtle body assumes all the roles: it is the perceiver, it is the instrument of perception, and it is also the object which is perceived.

स्वप्ने तु बुद्धि: स्वयमेव जाग्रत्-

कालीन-नानाविध-वासनाभि: ।

कर्त्रादिभावं प्रतिपद्य राजते

यत्र स्वयं भाति ह्ययं परात्मा ॥ ९८

Acquiring the sense of agency etc., the mind alone reigns in the dream state, along with the diverse desires from the waking state. The supreme self is here self-resplendent. (98)

> The Ātman's light (of consciousness) is more obvious in the dream state because, unlike in the waking state, there is no other source of light and, unlike in the deep sleep state, there *are* things to be perceived.

धीमात्रकोपाधिरशेषसाक्षी

न लिप्यते तत्कृतकर्मलेशै: ।

यस्मादसङ्गस्तत एव कर्मभि:

न लिप्यते किञ्चिदुपाधिना कृतै: ॥ ९९

The witness of everything is not affected by any work done by the mind, which is its only superimposition. Being unattached, the self is not affected by any work done by its superimpositions. (99)

सर्वव्यापृतिकरणं लिङ्गमिदं स्याच्चिदात्मन: पुंस: ।
वास्यादिकमिव तक्ष्णस्तेनैवात्मा भवत्यसङ्गोऽयम् ॥ १००

The subtle body is the instrument—like those of a carpenter—for all activities (apparently) done by the Ātman, which is pure consciousness. The Ātman is unattached. (100)

अन्धत्व-मन्दत्व-पटुत्व-धर्मा:
सौगुण्य-वैगुण्य-वशाद्धि चक्षुष: ।
बाधिर्य-मूकत्व-मुखास्तथैव
श्रोत्रादिधर्मा न तु वेत्तुरात्मन: ॥ १०१

Blindness, weakness and sharpness are conditions that belong to the eye and are due merely to its being healthy or defective. Deafness and dumbness are similarly conditions of the ear, etc. None of these belong to the Ātman, which is the knower. (101)

उच्छ्वास-नि:श्वास-विजृम्भणक्षुत्-
प्रस्यन्दनाद्युत्क्रमणादिका: क्रिया: ।
प्राणादि-कर्माणि वदन्ति तज्ज्ञा:
प्राणस्य धर्मावशनापिपासे ॥ १०२

Experts (in these matters) say that actions such as inhaling, exhaling, yawning, sneezing, secreting, and leaving the body belong to prāṇa and the rest. Hunger and thirst are (also) the characteristics of prāṇa. (102)

> The phrase "prāṇa and the rest" refers to the subdivisions within prāṇa (see #95), each of which is associated with a specific action of the type mentioned in the verse.

अन्तःकरणमेतेषु चक्षुरादिषु वर्ष्मणि ।
अहमित्यभिमानेन तिष्ठत्याभासतेजसा ॥ १०३

Filled with the reflection of consciousness (Ātman), the inner instrument (mind) dwells in the body and in the senses such as the eye, identifying with them as "I." (103)

अहंकारः स विज्ञेयः कर्ता भोक्ताभिमान्ययम् ।
सत्त्वादि-गुणयोगेन चावस्थात्रयमश्नुते ॥ १०४

Identifying itself as the doer and the experiencer, it (i.e. the mind) becomes known as the ego ("I-ness"). Being associated with the guṇas like *sattva,* it experiences the three states. (104)

> Although all the three guṇas are always present in the mind, it experiences the waking (*jāgrat*) state when *rajas* is dominant, the dream (*svapna*) state when *sattva* is dominant, and the deep sleep (*suṣupti*) state when *tamas* is dominant.

विषयाणामानुकूल्ये सुखी दुःखी विपर्यये ।
सुखं दुःखं च तद्धर्मः सदानन्दस्य नात्मनः ॥ १०५

When objects are favorable, it becomes happy; when not, it becomes sad. Joy and sorrow are characteristics of the mind, not of the ever-blissful Ātman. (105)

> The same object can produce joy at one time and sorrow at another, proving that joy and sorrow don't belong to the object but to the mind.

आत्मार्थत्वेन हि प्रेयान्विषयो न स्वत: प्रिय: ।

स्वत एव हि सर्वेषामात्मा प्रियतमो यत: ॥ १०६

Objects are not intrinsically lovable; they are loved for the sake of the self, since it is only the self that everyone loves for its own sake. (106)

तत आत्मा सदानन्दो नास्य दु:खं कदाचन ।

यत्सुषुप्तौ निर्विषय आत्मानन्दोऽनुभूयते ।

श्रुति: प्रत्यक्षमैतिह्यमनुमानं च जाग्रति ॥ १०७

The scripture (*śruti*), direct experience (*pratyakṣa*), tradition (*aitihya*), and inference (*anumāna*) validate the self's blissful experience independent of objects, which occurs in deep sleep. Therefore the Ātman is ever-blissful and never experiences sorrow. (107)

The causal body, which is none other than māyā, is now described:

अव्यक्तनाम्नी परमेशशक्ति:

अनाद्यविद्या त्रिगुणात्मिका परा ।

कार्यानुमेया सुधियैव माया

यया जगत्सर्वमिदं प्रसूयते ॥ १०८

Māyā or ignorance, known as "the unmanifest" (*avyakta*), is the power of the Supreme Ruler. She is without beginning (*anādi*), superior (as cause is to effects), and consists of the three *guṇas*. A person of clear intellect can know her existence only through its effects. It is from her that this whole universe has emerged. (108)

> The effects depend on their cause, hence the cause is thought of as "superior." Māyā's three attributes are called *guṇas*: *sattva, rajas* and *tamas*. They are described in #110-19.

सन्नाप्यसन्नाप्युभयात्मिका नो
भिन्नाप्यभिन्नाप्युभयात्मिका नो ।
साङ्गाप्यनङ्गा ह्युभयात्मिका नो
महाद्भुताऽनिर्वचनीयरूपा ॥ १०९

She is neither real nor unreal nor both, neither different (from) nor the same (as Brahman) nor both, and neither composed of parts nor without parts nor both. She is most amazing and indescribable. (109)

शुद्धाद्वयब्रह्म-विबोधनाश्या
सर्पभ्रमो रज्जु-विवेकतो यथा ।
रजस्तम:सत्वमिति प्रसिद्धा
गुणास्तदीया: प्रथितै: स्वकार्यै: ॥ ११०

Just as the delusion of a snake vanishes when the rope is discerned, so does māyā vanish when the pure, nondual Brahman is directly experienced. Māyā's attributes (*guṇa*)—*rajas, tamas and sattva*— are well known through their effects. (110)

विक्षेपशक्ती रजस: क्रियात्मिका

यत: प्रवृत्ति: प्रसृता पुराणी ।

रागादयोऽस्या: प्रभवन्ति नित्यं

दु:खादयो ये मनसो विकारा: ॥ १११

Rajas has projecting power (*vikṣepa-śakti*), which initiates action and from which emerges the primal creative activity. It continually produces mental modifications such as attachment (*rāga*) and grief (*duḥkha*). (111)

> The phrase, "from which emerges the primal creative activity," is a reference to the Gītā (15. 4).

काम: क्रोधो लोभ-दभाभ्यसूया-

अहंकारेष्याी-मत्सराद्यास्तु घोरा: ।

धर्मा एते राजसा: पुम्प्रवृत्ति:

यस्मादेषा तद्रजो बन्धहेतु: ॥ ११२

The dreadful qualities of *rajas*—like lust, anger, greed, arrogance, jealousy, egoism, envy, and spite—prompt a person's outgoing tendencies. Therefore *rajas* is a cause of bondage. (112)

एषाऽऽवृत्तिर्नाम तमोगुणस्य

शक्तिर्यया वस्त्ववभासतेऽन्यथा ।

सैषा निदानं पुरुषस्य संसृते:

विक्षेपशक्ते: प्रवणस्य हेतु: ॥ ११३

Tamas has veiling power (*āvaraṇa-śakti*), which makes an object appear different from what it is. It is the cause of a person's transmigration and activates the projecting power. (113)

प्रज्ञावानपि पण्डितोऽपि चतुरोऽप्यत्यन्तसूक्ष्मार्थदृग्-
व्यालीढस्तमसा न वेत्ति बहुधा संबोधितोऽपि स्फुटम् ।
भ्रान्त्यारोपितमेव साधु कलयत्यालम्बते तद्गुणान्
हन्तासौ प्रबला दुरन्त-तमस: शक्तिर्महत्यावृति: ॥ ११४

Even a person who is wise, learned, clever, and endowed with subtle perception is covered by *tamas* and may not understand the Ātman even when explained clearly. Such a person accepts as true whatever is superimposed through delusion (i.e., body and mind) and identifies with its qualities. Alas, how powerful is the great veiling power of the dreadful *tamas*! (114)

अभावना वा विपरीतभावना
संभावना विप्रतिपत्तिरस्या: ।
संसर्गयुक्तं न विमुञ्चति ध्रुवं
विक्षेपशक्ति: क्षपयत्यजस्रम् ॥ ११५

Whoever is affected by this (veiling power) is never freed from wrong thinking, contrary thinking, and confused or uncertain thinking. The projecting power always troubles such a person. (115)

अज्ञानमालस्य-जडत्व-निद्रा-
प्रमाद-मूढत्व-मुखास्तमोगुणा: ।

एतै: प्रयुक्तो नहि वेत्ति किंचित्
निद्रालुवत्स्तंभवदेव तिष्ठति ॥ ११६

Ignorance, laziness, dullness, sleep, unmindfulness, and stupidity
are among the attributes of *tamas*. A person endowed with these
qualities does not know anything, and remains like one asleep or
like a pillar. (116)

> Like a pillar or like someone asleep, such a person does not
> initiate any activity.

सत्त्वं विशुद्धं जलवत्तथापि
ताभ्यां मिलित्वा सरणाय कल्पते ।
यत्रात्मबिम्ब: प्रतिबिम्बित: सन्
प्रकाशयत्यर्क इवाखिलं जडम् ॥ ११७

Although *sattva* is pure like (clear) water, it combines with *rajas*
and *tamas* to generate this universe. The Ātman is reflected in
sattva and, like the sun, illumines the entire material universe. (117)

मिश्रस्य सत्त्वस्य भवन्ति धर्मा:
त्वमानिताद्या नियमा यमाद्या: ।
श्रद्धा च भक्तिश्च मुमुक्षुता च
दैवी च सम्पत्तिरसन्निवृत्ति: ॥ ११८

The qualities of mixed *sattva* are absence of pride, etc. (see Gītā, 13.
7–11), *niyama*, *yama*, faith, devotion, longing for freedom, the
divine attributes (Gītā, 16. 1-2), and withdrawal from the unreal.
(118)

Niyama includes cleanliness, contentment, austerity, study, and worship of God. *Yama* includes nonviolence, truthfulness, nonstealing, chastity, and non-receiving of gifts. (*Yoga-Sūtra*, 2. 30, 32)

विशुद्धसत्त्वस्य गुणा: प्रसाद:
स्वात्मानुभूति: परमा प्रशान्ति: ।
तृप्ति: प्रहर्ष: परमात्मनिष्ठा
यया सदानन्दरसं समृच्छति ॥ ११९

The qualities of pure *sattva* are cheerfulness, self-realization, supreme peace, contentment, bliss, supreme devotion to the Ātman, by which eternal bliss is attained. (119)

When *sattva* is present by itself, unmixed with *rajas* and *tamas,* it is "pure."

अव्यक्तमेतत्-त्रिगुणैर्निरुक्तं
तत्कारणं नाम शरीरमात्मन: ।
सुषुप्तिरेतस्य विभक्त्यवस्था
प्रलीनसर्वेन्द्रियबुद्धिवृत्ति: ॥ १२०

The unmanifest (*avyakta*), said to be comprised of the three *guṇas*, is the causal body (*kāraṇa śarīra*) of the Ātman. Deep sleep (*suṣupti*) is its special state, in which subside all the senses and the thought-waves (*vṛtti*) of the mind. (120)

The "special state" of the causal body is deep sleep, because that is where its presence becomes more obvious.

सर्वप्रकार-प्रमिति-प्रशान्ति:
बीजात्मनावस्थितिरेव बुद्धे: ।
सुषुप्तिरेतस्य किल प्रतीति:
किंचिन्न वेद्मीति जगत्प्रसिद्धे: ॥ १२१

All forms of knowing remain suspended in deep sleep and the mind exists only in a seed-form. This is proved by the universal experience: "I did not know anything then." (121)

The experience of not knowing anything in deep sleep is recollected upon waking.

देहेन्द्रिय-प्राण-मनोऽहमादय:
सर्वे विकारा विषया: सुखादय: ।
व्योमादि-भूतान्यखिलं च विश्वं
अव्यक्तपर्यन्तमिदं ह्यनात्मा ॥ १२२

The non-self (anātmā) comprises all material entities such as the body, the senses (indriya), the life-force (prāṇa), the mind, the ego, etc., the sense-objects (viṣaya), pleasure, etc., all primal elements such as space, in fact, the entire universe including the unmanifest. (122)

The "etc." after pleasure includes pain, delusion, envy, jealousy, and fear.

माया मायाकार्यं सर्वं महदादि-देहपर्यन्तम् ।
असदिदमनात्मतत्त्वं विद्धि त्वं मरु-मरीचिका-कल्पम् ॥ १२३

Know that māyā and all the effects of māyā, ranging from the cosmic intelligence to the gross body, are non-self, and unreal like a mirage in a desert. (123)

> Also known as the "golden womb" (*hiraṇyagarbha*), cosmic intelligence (*mahat*) is among the first to emerge from māyā. See Kaṭha Upaniṣad, 1.3.10-11.

How the Self Is Concealed

The nature of the Ātman is now explained (#124–36):

अथ ते संप्रवक्ष्यामि स्वरूपं परमात्मन: ।
यद्विज्ञाय नरो बन्धान्मुक्त: कैवल्यमश्नुते ॥ १२४

Now I will explain to you the nature of the supreme self, knowing which a person is freed from bondage and attains liberation. (124)

> This verse refers to liberation as "the state of being alone" (*kaivalya*), meaning, the infinite is all that exists.

The disciple's question, "Who is the supreme self?" (#49) *is answered in the following verses* 125–36:

अस्ति कश्चित्स्वयं नित्यमहंप्रत्ययलम्बन: ।
अवस्थात्रयसाक्षी सन्पञ्चकोशविलक्षण: ॥ १२५

There is someone independent, eternal, on whom the ego is projected, who is the witness of the three states and distinct from the five layers. (125)

The "three states" are waking, dream and deep sleep. The "five layers" are those of the body (lit. "food," *annamaya*), the life-force (*prāṇamaya*), the mind (*manomaya*), the agent ego (lit. "knowledge," *vijñānamaya*), and the experiencer ego (lit. "bliss," *ānandamaya*).

यो विजानाति सकलं जाग्रत्स्वप्नसुषुप्तिषु ।
बुद्धि-तद्वृत्ति-सद्भावमभावमहमित्ययम् ॥ १२६

(There is someone) who is aware of the presence and absence of the mind's activity and of everything that occurs in the states of waking, dream and deep sleep—this is that. (126)

See, for instance, Kena Upaniṣad (1.6) and Bṛhadāraṇyaka Upaniṣad (3.4.2).

य: पश्यति स्वयं सर्वं यं न पश्यति कश्चन ।
यश्चेतयति बुद्ध्यादि न तद्यं चेतयत्ययम् ॥ १२७

(There is someone) who sees everything but who is not seen by anyone, who illumines the mind etc. but whom they cannot illumine —this is that. (127)

The Ātman's consciousness is reflected in the mind and the body ("who illumines the mind etc."), which makes them appear conscious.

येन विश्वमिदं व्याप्तं यं न व्याप्नोति किञ्चन ।
आभारूपमिदं सर्वं यं भान्तमनुभात्ययम् ॥ १२८

(There is someone) who pervades this universe but nothing pervades it, whose shining precedes the experience of this material universe—this is that. (128)

यस्य सन्निधिमात्रेण देहेन्द्रियमनोधिय: ।
विषयेषु स्वकीयेषु वर्तन्ते प्रेरिता इव ॥ १२९

(There is someone) whose mere proximity seems to direct the body, the senses, the mind, and the intellect towards their objects (—this is that.) (129)

अहङ्कारादि-देहान्ता विषयाश्च सुखादय: ।
वेद्यन्ते घटवद् येन नित्यबोध-स्वरूपिणा ॥ १३०

Everything ranging from the ego to the body, as well as the experience of happiness etc., are perceived as an object by this whose nature is eternal consciousness (—this is that.) (130)

एषोऽन्तरात्मा पुरुष: पुराणो
निरन्तराखण्ड-सुखानुभूति: ।
सदैकरूप: प्रतिबोधमात्रो
येनेषिता वागसवश्चरन्ति ॥ १३१

This indwelling Being is the inner self—ancient, of the nature of continuous and infinite bliss, ever the same, present in every experience, and whose ruling makes speech and other senses do their functions. (131)

अत्रैव सत्त्वात्मनि धीगुहायां
अव्याकृताकाश उशत्प्रकाश: ।
आकाश उच्चै रविवत्प्रकाशते
स्वतेजसा विश्वमिदं प्रकाशयन् ॥ १३२

Illumining this whole universe by its own light, the Ātman shines like the midday sun with its bright effulgence, (1) here in the body, (2) in the pure mind which is the cave of heart, and (3) in the undifferentiated space. (132)

> The Ātman illumines not only the external world but also the gross body, the subtle body ("the pure mind which is the cave of the heart") and the causal body ("undifferentiated space").

ज्ञाता मनोऽहंकृतिविक्रियाणां
देहेन्द्रियप्राणकृतक्रियाणाम् ।
अयोऽग्निवत्ताननुवर्तमानो
न चेष्टते नो विकरोति किञ्चन ॥ १३३

The Ātman is the knower of the changes in the mind and the ego, and of the activities of the body, the senses and the prāṇa. Like fire in a piece of iron, it neither does anything nor is transformed in any way. (133)

> The presence of fire turns a piece of iron red hot, but the fire itself neither engages in any activity nor has a form of its own and is not transformed in any way.

न जायते नो म्रियते न वर्धते

न क्षीयते नो विकरोति नित्य: ।

विलीयमानेऽपि वपुष्यमुष्मिन्

न लीयते कुम्भ इवाम्बरं स्वयम् ॥ १३४

The Ātman is eternal: it is not born, it does not die, it does not grow, it does not decay, and it does not change. The Ātman is independent: it is not destroyed when the body is destroyed, just as the space inside a jar is not destroyed when the jar is destroyed. (134)

प्रकृति-विकृति-भिन्न: शुद्धबोध-स्वभाव:

सदसदिदमशेषं भासयन्निर्विशेष: ।

विलसति परमात्मा जाग्रदादिष्ववस्थासु

अहमहमिति साक्षात्साक्षिरूपेण बुद्धे: ॥ १३५

The supreme Ātman is distinct from the material cause (*prakṛti*) and its effects. Its nature is pure consciousness, it is free from attributes, and it illumines the entire gross and subtle universe. In the waking and other states it manifests directly as "I", the witness of the intellect. (135)

> Every object is perceived only when we become conscious of it. But consciousness does *not* need an object for its own existence. It is independent and can exist on its own. Such objectless consciousness is considered "pure" (*śuddha*).

नियमितमनसामुं त्वं स्वमात्मानमात्मनि

अयमहमिति साक्षाद्विद्धि बुद्धिप्रसादात् ।

जनि-मरण-तरंगापार-संसारसिन्धुं
प्रतर भव कृतार्थो ब्रह्मरूपेण संस्थ: ॥ १३६

With the help of a disciplined mind and a purified intellect, experience the Ātman directly to be your own self. Cross this unbounded ocean of saṁsāra, whose waves are birth and death, and become fulfilled by dwelling securely in Brahman-consciousness. (136)

The disciple's question, "What is bondage?" (#49), is answered in the following two verses (137–38):

अत्रानात्मन्यहमिति मतिर्बन्ध एषोऽस्य पुंस:
प्राप्तोऽज्ञानाज्जनन-मरण-क्लेश-संपातहेतु: ।
येनैवायं वपुरिदमसत्सत्यमित्यात्मबुद्ध्या
पुष्यत्युक्षत्यवति विषयैस्तन्तुभि: कोशकृद्वत् ॥ १३७

Identifying with the non-self as "I" is bondage. This is caused by ignorance and it immerses a person in the suffering caused by birth and death. Seeing this perishable body as "I" and (therefore) real, the person nourishes it, bathes it, and protects it with sense objects —and gets trapped like a caterpillar in its cocoon. (137)

अतस्मिंस्तद्बुद्धि: प्रभवति विमूढस्य तमसा
विवेकाभावाद्वै स्फुरति भुजगे रज्जुधिषणा ।
ततोऽनर्थव्रातो निपतति समादातुरधिक:
ततो योऽसद्ग्राह: स हि भवति बन्ध: शृणु सखे ॥ १३८

Due to ignorance, the deluded sees a thing that is not there. The absence of discernment leads to seeing a rope instead of a snake, and one who grasps it experiences great suffering. Listen: this kind of taking one thing for another, my friend, is itself bondage. (138)

> The reference is to the example of a coiled rope mistaken for a snake in a partially lit room.

The disciple's question—how did the bondage arise? (#49)—is answered in the following verses (139–44):

अखण्डनित्याद्वयबोधशक्त्या
स्फुरन्तमात्मानमनन्तवैभवम् ।
समावृणोत्यावृतिशक्तिरेषा
तमोमयी राहुरिवार्कबिम्बम् ॥ १३९

The infinite glory of the Ātman, which shines with the power of the indivisible, eternal and nondual consciousness, is covered by the concealing power of ignorance, the way the sun is covered by Rāhu. (139)

> The reference is to the solar eclipse. In Indian mythology, the sun is said to be periodically covered by a demon named Rāhu.

तिरोभूते स्वात्मन्यमलतरतेजोवति पुमान्
अनात्मानं मोहादहमिति शरीरं कलयति ।
ततः काम-क्रोध-प्रभृतिभिरमुं बन्धनगुणैः
परं विक्षेपाख्या रजस उरुशक्ति-व्यथयति ॥ १४०

The deluded person sees the body, which is not the self, as "I" when the true self, which is pure consciousness, is covered. The fierce power of *rajas,* known as the projecting power, then inflicts great suffering through bondage-producing qualities such as lust and anger. (140)

महामोह-ग्रासग्रसन-गलितात्मावगमनो
धियो नानावस्थां स्वयमभिनयंस्तद्गुणतया ।
अपारे संसारे विषयविषपूरे जलनिधौ
निमज्योन्मज्यायं भ्रमति कुमतिः कुत्सितगतिः ॥ १४१

Set in a wrong direction with an unfit mind, a person whose self-knowledge has been swallowed by the crocodile of great delusion, superimposes on the self the various states of the mind and, identifying with them, drifts up and down in this boundless ocean of saṁsāra, which is filled with poisonous material objects. (141)

भानुप्रभा-संजनिताभ्रपङ्क्तिः
भानुं तिरोधाय विजृम्भते यथा ।
आत्मोदिताहंकृतिरात्मतत्त्वं
तथा तिरोधाय विजृम्भते स्वयम् ॥ १४२

Just as a cluster of clouds, produced by the sun's rays, covers the sun and appears (in the sky), so does the "I"-sense, produced by the Ātman, cover the Ātman and appear by itself. (142)

कबलितदिननाथे दुर्दिने सान्द्रमेघैः
व्यथयति हिमझंझा-वायुरुग्रो यथैतान् ।

अविरत-तमसात्मन्यावृते मूढबुद्धिं
क्षपयति बहुदु:खै-स्तीव्रविक्षेपशक्ति: ॥ १४३

When the sun is completely covered by dense clouds on some
terrible day, a fierce wind with freezing rain causes suffering. In the
same way, when the Ātman is covered by unceasing ignorance, the
fierce projecting power afflicts the deluded person with profuse
misery. (143)

एताभ्यामेव शक्तिभ्यां बन्ध: पुंस: समागत: ।
याभ्यां विमोहितो देहं मत्वाऽऽत्मानं भ्रमत्ययम् ॥ १४४

It is from these two powers that a person's bondage has emerged,
deluded by which the person looks upon the body as "I" and
wanders (in the vicious circle of saṁsāra). (144)

The disciple's question (#49)—how does bondage exist?—is answered in the
following two verses (145–46):

बीजं संसृतिभूमिजस्य तु तमो देहात्मधीरङ्कुरो
राग: पल्लवमम्बु कर्म तु वपु: स्कन्धोऽसव: शाखिका: ।
अग्राणीन्द्रियसंहतिश्च विषया: पुष्पाणि दु:खं फलं
नानाकर्म-समुद्भवं बहुविधं भोक्तात्र जीव: खग: ॥ १४५

The tree of saṁsāra has ignorance as its seed. Its sprout is the
awareness of the body as "I", attachment its tender leaves, karma its
water, body its trunk, the prāṇa its branches, the senses its twigs,
and the sense objects its flowers. Its fruits are different kinds of

misery resulting from diverse karmas, feasting on which is the
embodied self (*jīva*) as the bird. (145)

> The imagery of the *jīva* as a bird feasting on the fruits of karma is
> found in the Muṇḍaka Upaniṣad (3.1.1-2).

अज्ञानमूलोऽयमनात्मबन्धो

नैसर्गिकोऽनादिरनन्त ईरितः ।

जन्माप्यय-व्याधि-जरादिदुःख-

प्रवाहपातं जनयत्यमुष्य ॥ १४६

Rooted in ignorance, this binding identification with what is not the
real self is said to be natural, without beginning and without end. It
generates the flow of misery caused by factors such as birth, death,
disease, and old age. (146)

> It is "natural" because its cause (prior mental impressions) is
> known. It is "without beginning" because no one can say *when* it
> began. It is "without end" *unless* knowledge of the real self dawns.

The disciple's question, "How is freedom attained?" (#49), is answered in the
following two verses (147–48):

नास्त्रैर्न शस्त्रैरनिलेन वह्निना

छेत्तुं न शक्यो न च कर्मकोटिभिः ।

विवेक-विज्ञान-महासिना विना

धातुः प्रसादेन शितेन मञ्जुना ॥ १४७

It is not possible to destroy this bondage with missiles or with
weapons or with wind or with fire or with millions of acts. It cannot

be done without the amazingly mighty sword of discerning knowledge, which is sharpened through the purity of the senses. (147)

> Bondage is a product of ignorance and hence it can be destroyed only through knowledge, not through karma, even if the karma is enjoined by the scriptures.

श्रुतिप्रमाणैकमते: स्वधर्म-

निष्ठा तयैवात्मविशुद्धिरस्य ।

विशुद्धबुद्धे: परमात्मवेदनं

तेनैव संसार-समूलनाश: ॥ १४८

A single-minded dedication to the Vedas leads to commitment to one's duties which, in turn, leads to purification of the mind. One whose mind is pure experiences the supreme self which, in turn, destroys saṁsāra along with its roots. (148)

Five Layers

We have seen how the Ātman can be viewed as covered by three bodies (#72-123). Another way to imagine the Ātman's concealment is to think of it as covered by five layers (kośa), each of which—like the three bodies—is mistaken for the Ātman due to ignorance.

The meaning of "you" (tvam) in the Upaniṣadic statement, "You are that" (tat tvam asi) is examined in the following verses by analyzing the five layers. These verses answer the disciple's question, "How is discernment practiced between the self and the non-self?" (#49).

कोशैरन्नमयाद्यै: पञ्चभिरात्मा न संवृतो भाति ।

निजशक्ति-समुत्पन्नै: शैवालपटलैरिवाम्बु वापीस्थम् ॥ १४९

69

Blanketed by the five layers—such as the layer of food (*annamaya*) —which arise from its own power, the Ātman remains hidden, just like the water in a pond remains hidden by the moss. (149)

> The term *anna* (lit. "food") is often used in Vedānta texts to refer to matter. Here it refers to the visible part of our personality, the body, which is sustained by food.

तच्छैवालापनये सम्यक् सलिलं प्रतीयते शुद्धम् ।
तृष्णा-सन्तापहरं सद्य: सौख्यप्रदं परं पुंस: ॥ १५०

The pure water which takes away the pangs of thirst and brings immediate joy is seen clearly when the moss is removed. (150)

पञ्चानामपि कोशानामपवादे विभात्ययं शुद्ध: ।
नित्यानन्दैकरस: प्रत्यग्रूप: पर: स्वयंज्योति: ॥ १५१

The Ātman—who is pure, eternal and unalloyed bliss, indwelling, supreme, and self-effulgent—shines when all the five layers are removed. (151)

आत्मानात्मविवेक: कर्तव्यो बन्धमुक्तये विदुषा ।
तेनैवानन्दी भवति स्वं विज्ञाय सच्चिदानन्दम् ॥ १५२

In order to be free from bondage, the wise should practice discernment between the Ātman and the non-self. It is only this that brings happiness through the knowledge of the self, who is being (*sat*), consciousness (*cit*) and bliss (*ānanda*). (152)

मुञ्जादिषीकामिव दृश्यवर्गात्
प्रत्यञ्चमात्मानमसङ्गमक्रियम् ।
विविच्य तत्र प्रविलाप्य सर्वं
तदात्मना तिष्ठति यः स मुक्तः ॥ १५३

A person attains freedom by discerning the indwelling, unattached, and inactive Ātman from the sense objects—the way a stalk of grass is separated from its covering sheath—and, after merging everything in the Ātman, remains identified with it. (153)

> The Ātman is "inactive" (*akriya*). All activity occurs in the layers, not in the Ātman.

The layer of food (annamaya kośa) is now described (#154-64):

देहोऽयमन्नभवनोऽन्नमयस्तु कोशश्च
अन्नेन जीवति विनश्यति तद्विहीनः ।
त्वक्-चर्म-मांस-रुधिरास्थि-पुरीष-राशिः
नायं स्वयं भवितुमर्हति नित्यशुद्धः ॥ १५४

This body is the layer of food (*annamaya*). A product of food, it is also sustained by food and destroyed without it. It is a mass of skin, flesh, blood, bones and filth. It cannot be the eternally pure Ātman. (154)

पूर्वं जनेरधिमृतेरपि नायमस्ति
जातक्षणः क्षणगुणोऽनियतस्वभावः ।
नैको जडश्च घटवत्परिदृश्यमानः
स्वात्मा कथं भवति भावविकारवेत्ता ॥ १५५

The body exists neither before birth nor after death, but only for a short time. Its traits are transitory and its nature is changeful. Like a jar, it is divisible, inert and perceivable. How can it be the Ātman, who is the witness of all changes? (155)

पाणिपादादिमान्देहो नात्मा व्यङ्गेऽपि जीवनात् ।
तत्तच्छक्तेरनाशाच्च न नियम्यो नियामक: ॥ १५६

The body is not the Ātman since it can live even without its limbs such as arms and legs, and since their functions remain unimpeded. The one who is the controller (*Ātman*) cannot be the one who is controlled (*body*). (156)

> While one or more limbs may be absent or nonfunctional, other limbs continue to function as expected.

देह-तद्धर्म-तत्कर्म-तदवस्थादि-साक्षिण: ।
सत एव स्वत:सिद्धं तद्वैलक्षण्यमात्मन: ॥ १५७

Being the witness of the body and of its attributes, activities and states, the Ātman makes its distinction (from the body) self-evident. (157)

शल्यराशि-मांसलिप्तो मलपूर्णो ऽतिकश्मल: ।
कथं भवेदयं वेत्ता स्वयमेतद्विलक्षण: ॥ १५८

The body is (1) a bunch of bones, (2) covered with flesh, (3) filled with filth, and (4) extremely impure. How can it be the Ātman, who is the knower distinct from the body? (158)

त्वङ्-मांस-मेदोऽस्थि-पुरीषराशौ
अहंमतिं मूढजन: करोति ।
विलक्षणं वेत्ति विचारशीलो
निजस्वरूपं परमार्थभूतम् ॥ १५९

A collection of skin, flesh, fat, bones, and filth is what a fool thinks of as "I". A thoughtful person knows the nature of the Ātman to be different (from the body) and absolutely real. (159)

देहोऽहमित्येव जडस्य बुद्धि:
देहे च जीवे विदुषस्त्वहंधी: ।
विवेकविज्ञानवतो महात्मनो
ब्रह्माहमित्येव मति: सदात्मनि ॥ १६०

A stupid person thinks of the body as "I". A scholar thinks of both the body as well as the embodied self (*jīva*) as "I". The great soul who has discerning knowledge always thinks of the Ātman as "I am the infinite (*Brahman*)." (160)

> A "scholar" who has indirect (or theoretical) knowledge (1) thinks of the body as "I" in matters of the present life and (2) thinks of the embodied self as "I" in matters of the afterlife. The "great soul" is the illumined one who directly experiences the reality and sees the "I" as infinite.

अत्रात्मबुद्धिं त्यज मूढबुद्धे
त्वङ्-मांस-मेदोऽस्थि-पुरीष-राशौ ।

सर्वात्मनि ब्रह्मणि निर्विकल्पे

कुरुष्व शांतिं परमां भजस्व ॥ १६१

O foolish one! Give up thinking of this cluster of skin, flesh, fat, bones, and filth as "I" and think of the self of all, Brahman, as "I" and thus attain supreme peace. (161)

देहेन्द्रियादावसति भ्रमोदितां

विद्वानहंतां न जहाति यावत् ।

तावन्न तस्यास्ति विमुक्तिवार्तापि

अस्त्वेष वेदान्तनयान्तदर्शी ॥ १६२

As long as the scholar does not give up the deluded sense of "I" in unreal entities such as the body and the senses, there is no possibility of freedom, even if the person is an expert in Vedānta philosophy. (162)

छायाशरीरे प्रतिबिम्बगात्रे

यत्स्वप्नदेहे हृदि कल्पिताङ्गे ।

यथात्मबुद्धिस्तव नास्ति काचित्

जीवच्छरीरे च तथैव माऽस्तु ॥ १६३

Just as you have no sense of "I" in the shadow of your body, or in the reflection of your body, or in your body in the dream state, or in the body of your imagination, so should you not have it in your body in the waking state. (163)

देहात्मधीरेव नृणामसद्धियां

जन्मादिदुःख-प्रभवस्य बीजम् ।

यतस्ततस्त्वं जहि तां प्रयत्नात्

त्यक्ते तु चित्ते न पुनर्भवाशा ॥ १६४

Since thinking of the body as "I" is itself the seed that produces the suffering of birth etc. in people whose hearts are attached to the unreal, you should make effort to destroy that sort of thinking. When that is removed from the mind, there is no chance of rebirth. (164)

> By "birth etc." is meant the six stages of life: birth, growth, transformation, decay, disease, and death.

The layer of prāṇa (prāṇamaya kośa) is now described (#165-66):

कर्मेन्द्रियैः पञ्चभिरञ्चितोऽयं

प्राणो भवेत्प्राणमयस्तु कोशः ।

येनात्मवानन्नमयोऽनुपूर्णः

प्रवर्ततेऽसौ सकलक्रियासु ॥ १६५

The layer of prāṇa (*prāṇamaya*) consists of prāṇa along with the five senses of action. Permeated by the layer of prāṇa as (if it were) the self, the layer of food engages in all activities. (165)

> The five senses of action are those which control speech, manual activity, locomotion, excretion and reproduction. See #92.

नैवात्मापि प्राणमयो वायु-विकारो

गन्ताऽऽगन्ता वायुवदन्तर्बहिरेषः ।

यस्मात्किञ्चित्क्वापि न वेत्तीष्टमनिष्टं

स्वं वान्यं वा किञ्चन नित्यं परतन्त्रः ॥ १६६

The layer of prāṇa also is not the Ātman, because it is a modification of prāṇa and, like the air (we breathe), it moves in and out, it doesn't know anything at all about what is good or bad for itself or for others, and it is forever dependent (on the Ātman). (166)

The layer of the mind (manomaya kośa) is now described (#167-83):

ज्ञानेन्द्रियाणि च मनश्च मनोमय: स्यात्
कोशो ममाहमिति वस्तुविकल्प-हेतु: ।
संज्ञादिभेदकलनाकलितो बलीयान्
तत्पूर्वकोशमभिपूर्य विजृम्भते य: ॥ १६७

The layer of the mind consists of the mind along with the five senses of knowledge. It is distinguished by its ability to ascribe names and forms to things and is the cause of characterizing them as "I" or "mine." It is powerful and does its function by permeating the previous layer (i.e. the layer of prāṇa). (167)

For the "five senses of knowledge," see #92.

पञ्चेन्द्रियै: पञ्चभिरेव होतृभि:
प्रचीयमानो विषयाज्यधारया ।
जाज्वल्यमानो बहुवासनेन्धनै:
मनोमयाग्निर्दहति प्रपञ्चम् ॥ १६८

The fire of the layer of the mind—which is tended with the fuel of numerous desires by the five senses, who serve as five priests, and set ablaze with the ghee-stream of sense objects—burns the universe. (168)

Limited by the senses and trapped by desires, people suffer due to the "burning" universe.

न ह्यस्त्यविद्या मनसोऽतिरिक्ता
मनो ह्यविद्या भवबन्ध-हेतुः ।
तस्मिन्विनष्टे सकलं विनष्टं
विजृम्भितेऽस्मिन्सकलं विजृम्भते ॥ १६९

There is no ignorance apart from the mind. The mind itself is ignorance, the cause of bondage of this world. When the mind disappears, everything disappears; when it manifests, everything becomes manifest. (169)

The mind disappears in deep sleep and merges in its cause, ignorance. When the mind manifests, the waking world or the dream world becomes manifest.

स्वप्नेऽर्थशून्ये सृजति स्वशक्त्या
भोक्त्रादिविश्वं मन एव सर्वम् ।
तथैव जाग्रत्यपि नो विशेषः
तत्सर्वमेतन्मनसो विजृम्भणम् ॥ १७०

In the dream state, when there is no contact with anything external, the mind alone, with its own power, projects the world consisting of the experiencer etc. It is no different in the waking state as well. All of this is the projection of the mind. (170)

The experiencer, the objects of experience, and the experience itself are all projected by the mind.

सुषुप्तिकाले मनसि प्रलीने
नैवास्ति किञ्चित्सकलप्रसिद्धे: ।
अतो मन:कल्पित एव पुंस:
संसार एतस्य न वस्तुतोऽस्ति ॥ १७१

It is well known to all that in deep sleep, when the mind subsides, there is nothing whatsoever. Hence this saṁsāra is only in the person's mind and is not real. (171)

वायुनाऽऽनीयते मेघ: पुनस्तेनैव नीयते ।
मनसा कल्प्यते बन्धो मोक्षस्तेनैव कल्पते ॥ १७२

The bondage is imagined by the mind and freedom is also imagined by the mind, just as a cloud is brought by the wind and is also carried away by the wind. (172)

देहादिसर्वविषये परिकल्प्य रागं
बध्नाति तेन पुरुषं पशुवद्गुणेन ।
वैरस्यमत्र विषवत् सुविधाय पश्चात्
एनं विमोचयति तन्मन एव बन्धात् ॥ १७३

Generating attachment to the body and all sense objects, the mind binds a person the way a rope binds an animal. It is the mind, again, that frees the person from the bondage by generating an aversion for them all as if they were poison. (173)

तस्मान्मन: कारणमस्य जन्तो:
बन्धस्य मोक्षस्य च वा विधाने ।

बन्धस्य हेतुर्मलिनं रजोगुणै:
मोक्षस्य शुद्धं विरजस्तमस्कम् ॥ १७४

Therefore it is the mind that is the cause of generating both bondage and freedom of all beings. The impure mind filled with elements of *rajas* is the cause of bondage, and the pure mind free from *rajas* and *tamas* is the cause of freedom. (174)

How does the mind become pure?

विवेक-वैराग्य-गुणातिरेकात्
शुद्धत्वमासाद्य मनो विमुक्त्यै ।
भवत्यतो बुद्धिमतो मुमुक्षो:
ताभ्यां दृढाभ्यां भवितव्यमग्रे ॥ १७५

Acquiring purity through intense discernment and detachment, the mind becomes the cause of freedom. Therefore the wise person who longs for freedom must first strengthen these two. (175)

मनो नाम महाव्याघ्रो विषयारण्यभूमिषु ।
चरत्यत्र न गच्छन्तु साधवो ये मुमुक्षव: ॥ १७६

The mind is a fierce tiger prowling in the forest of the sensual world. Spiritual seekers who long for freedom should keep away from it. (176)

मन: प्रसूते विषयानशेषान्
स्थूलात्मना सूक्ष्मतया च भोक्तु: ।

शरीर-वर्णाश्रम-जाति-भेदान्

गुण-क्रिया-हेतु-फलानि नित्यम् ॥ १७७

The mind continually produces for the experiencer innumerable sense objects, gross and subtle—the kinds of species, caste, stage of life, tribe, quality, activity, means, and results. (177)

> The mind conjures up objects, gross and subtle (in waking and dream states) of all kinds—species (human, animal, celestial), caste (trade affiliation), stage of life (student, householder, etc.), tribe (social grouping), quality (sound, touch, etc.), activity, means (instruments of action), and results (of action).

असङ्गचिद्रूपममुं विमोह्य

देहेन्द्रियप्राणगुणैर्निबद्ध्य ।

अहंममेति भ्रमयत्यजस्रं

मन: स्वकृत्येषु फलोपभुक्तिषु ॥ १७८

The Ātman, who is unattached consciousness, is deluded by the mind and bound with the ties of body, senses and prāṇa, identifying with them as "I" or "mine," and made to wander in order to experience the varied results of its actions. (178)

> It is attachment (showing up as "I" and "mine") that apparently binds the Ātman to the body, the senses, and prāṇa.

अध्यासदोषात्पुरुषस्य संसृति:

अध्यासबन्धस्त्वमुनैव कल्पित: ।

रजस्तमोदोषवतोऽविवेकिनो

जन्मादिदु:खस्य निदानमेतत् ॥ १७९

A person's fall into saṁsāra occurs due to the error of superimposition (*adhyāsa*). It is the non-discerning person's mind, tainted by *rajas* and *tamas,* that conjures up the bondage of superimposition and becomes the cause of suffering due to birth etc. (179)

> By "birth etc." is meant the six stages of life: birth, growth, transformation, decay, disease, and death. (see also #258)

अत: प्राहुर्मनोऽविद्यां पण्डितास्तत्त्वदर्शिन: ।
येनैव भ्राम्यते विश्वं वायुनेवाभ्रमण्डलम् ॥ १८०

That is why the wise, who perceive the truth, say that ignorance is the mind, which alone moves the universe here and there, like the wind which moves masses of clouds. (180)

> Being a product of ignorance, the mind is not different from ignorance and is the direct cause of saṁsāra.

तन्मन:शोधनं कार्यं प्रयत्नेन मुमुक्षुणा ।
विशुद्धे सति चैतस्मिन्मुक्ति: करफलायते ॥ १८१

One who longs for freedom should make earnest effort to purify the mind. When the mind is purified, freedom becomes as tangible as a fruit in one's hand. (181)

मोक्षैकसक्त्या विषयेषु रागं
निर्मूल्य संन्यस्य च सर्वकर्म ।
सच्छ्रद्धया य: श्रवणादिनिष्ठो
रज:स्वभावं स धुनोति बुद्धे: ॥ १८२

Getting rid of attachment to sense objects by single-minded longing for freedom and giving up all work, one who is faithfully devoted to the practice of hearing etc. destroys the impurities of the mind. (182)

> Giving up "work" means to stop thinking of oneself as the agent of work (*kartā*). The "practice of hearing etc." is a reference to the threefold practice of hearing (*śravaṇa*) the truth, reflecting (*manana*) on it, and meditating (*nididhyāsana*) on it.

मनोमयो नापि भवेत्परात्मा

ह्याद्यन्तवत्त्वात्-परिणामिभावात् ।

दु:खात्मकत्वात्-विषयत्वहेतो:

द्रष्टा हि दृश्यात्मतया न दृष्ट: ॥ १८३

The layer of the mind also cannot be the supreme self because (1) it begins and it ends, (2) it is changeable, (3) it is the cause of suffering, and, (4) because it is an object of perception, the perceiver cannot be identified as the perceived. (183)

> Unlike the supreme self, the mind's existence is not timeless: the mind is present in waking and dream but not in deep sleep, and its contents (such as desires and hopes) keep changing.

The layer of knowledge (vijñānamaya kośa) is now described (#184-206):

बुद्धिबुद्धीन्द्रियै: सार्धं सवृत्ति: कर्तृलक्षण: ।

विज्ञानमयकोश: स्यात्पुंस: संसारकारणम् ॥ १८४

The layer of knowledge, which endows agency, is the mind with its modification and the senses of knowledge—and it is the cause of the person's saṁsāra. (184)

> The layer of knowledge "endows agency" through the knowledge of being the agent. It is really the layer of the "ego as the doer (kartā)."

अनुव्रजच्चित्रतिबिम्बशक्ति:
विज्ञानसंज्ञ: प्रकृतेर्विकार: ।
ज्ञानक्रियावानहमित्यजस्रं
देहेन्द्रियादिष्वभिमन्यते भृशम् ॥ १८५

This layer of knowledge is a material product, empowered by the reflection of consciousness which accompanies it. It always identifies itself intensely with the body, the senses etc., and is endowed with the functions of knowledge and action. (185)

अनादिकालोऽयमहंस्वभावो
जीव: समस्तव्यवहारवोढा ।
करोति कर्माण्यनुपूर्ववासन:
पुण्यान्यपुण्यानि च तत्फलानि ॥ १८६
भुङ्क्ते विचित्रास्वपि योनिषु व्रजन्
आयाति निर्यात्यध ऊर्ध्वमेष: ।
अस्यैव विज्ञानमयस्य जाग्रत्-
स्वप्नाद्यवस्था: सुखदु:खभोग: ॥ १८७

Known as the jīva, it is without beginning and identifies itself as "I." It carries out all activities. Filled with desires from the past, it does things that are enjoined as well as those that are prohibited, and reaps their results. For that, it passes through diverse births, going up and coming down. It is this layer of knowledge that experiences waking, dream and other states, as also joy and sorrow. (186-87)

> The layer of knowledge is said to be "without beginning" because no one knows *when* it actually began. The "desires from the past" spring from the mental impressions produced by the past actions in this life as well as earlier lives. "Going up" refers to favorable births in heavenly worlds and "coming down" refers to unfavorable births in hellish worlds.

देहादिनिष्ठाश्रम-धर्म-कर्म-
गुणाभिमान: सततं ममेति ।
विज्ञानकोशोऽयमतिप्रकाश:
प्रकृष्टसान्निध्यवशात्परात्मन: ।
अतो भवत्येष उपाधिरस्य
यदात्मधी: संसरति भ्रमेण ॥ १८८

It always identifies with the duties, activities and characteristics related to the life's stages, which belong to the body. The layer of knowledge is highly effulgent because of its close proximity to the supreme self, which through delusion views the layer as "I" and suffers transmigration. (188)

योऽयं विज्ञानमय: प्राणेषु हृदि स्फुरत्स्वयंज्योति: ।
कूटस्थ: सन्नात्मा कर्ता भोक्ता भवत्युपाधिस्थ: ॥ १८९

The self-effulgent Ātman, whose essence is consciousness, shines in the heart and through the senses. Though immutable, it becomes the doer and the experiencer owing to its superimposed identity. (189)

स्वयं परिच्छेदमुपेत्य बुद्धे:
तादात्म्यदोषेण परं मृषात्मन: ।
सर्वात्मक: सन्नपि वीक्षते स्वयं
स्वत: पृथक्त्वेन मृदो घटानिव ॥ १९०

Though being the self of all, the Ātman acquires limitations by identifying itself with the false "I" of the layer of knowledge and sees itself as different, as the clay might do when seeing jars made from itself. (190)

उपाधिसम्बन्धवशात्परात्मा
ह्युपाधिधर्माननुभाति तद्गुण: ।
अयोविकारानविकारिवह्निवत्
सदैकरूपोऽपि पर: स्वभावात् ॥ १९१

Though being eternally transcendent and unchanging, the supreme self takes the form of the superimposed identity due to superimposition, like fire (though formless) takes the form of the iron which it turns red hot. (191)

॥ शिष्य उवाच ॥
भ्रमेणाप्यन्यथा वाऽस्तु जीवभाव: परात्मन: ।
तदुपाधेरनादित्वान्नानादेर्नाश इष्यते ॥ १९२

The disciple said:

The supreme self may see itself as the jīva through delusion or some other way. Since its superimposition has no beginning (#186), it cannot be said to have an end. (192)

अतोऽस्य जीवभावोऽपि नित्यो भवति संसृति: ।
न निवर्तेत तन्मोक्ष: कथं मे श्रीगुरो वद ॥ १९३

That makes the jīva identity also eternal, which means the saṁsāra can never end. How then will I attain freedom?—please tell me this, revered teacher. (193)

॥ श्रीगुरुरुवाच ॥
सम्यक्पृष्टं त्वया विद्वन्सावधानेन तच्छृणु ।
प्रामाणिकी न भवति भ्रान्त्या मोहितकल्पना ॥ १९४

The teacher said:

O wise one! Your question is appropriate. Listen to this carefully. The identity of a deluded person is caused by error and is not confirmed as real. (194)

भ्रान्तिं विना त्वसङ्गस्य निष्क्रियस्य निराकृते: ।
न घटेतार्थसम्बन्धो नभसो नीलतादिवत् ॥ १९५

Unattached, formless and beyond activity, the self cannot connect with any object without being deluded, as in the case of the sky and its blue color. (195)

Only under delusion is the sky seen as blue. The blueness of the sky seems inseparable from it until we know that it does not belong to the sky. Similarly the jīva nature of the self seems inseparable from it until we know that it does not belong to the self.

स्वस्य द्रष्टुर्निगुणस्याक्रियस्य
प्रत्यग्बोधानन्दरूपस्य बुद्धे: ।
भ्रान्त्या प्राप्तो जीवभावो न सत्यो
मोहापाये नास्त्यवस्तुस्वभावात् ॥ १९६

The Ātman is the witness, beyond qualities and activities, and its nature is inner awareness and bliss. Its jīva identity, resulting from the superimposition of the intellect, is not real. Being unreal by nature, it vanishes when the delusion is destroyed. (196)

यावद्भ्रान्तिस्तावदेवास्य सत्ता
मिथ्याज्ञानोज्जृम्भितस्य प्रमादात् ।
रज्ज्वां सर्पो भ्रान्तिकालीन एव
भ्रान्तेर्नाशे नैव सर्पो ऽपि तद्वत् ॥ १९७

Produced by an error due to false perception, the jīva's apparent existence lasts only as long as there is delusion. This is like the snake which is perceived instead of a rope only during the state of delusion. When the delusion ends, there is no snake. (197)

अनादित्वमविद्याया: कार्यस्यापि तथेष्यते ।
उत्पन्नायां तु विद्यायामाविद्यकमनाद्यपि ॥ १९८
प्रबोधे स्वप्नवत्सर्वं सहमूलं विनश्यति ।
अनाद्यपीदं नो नित्यं प्रागभाव इव स्फुटम् ॥ १९९

Ignorance being without beginning, its effect must also be likewise. Nevertheless, when knowledge dawns, all effects of ignorance, even if without beginning, disappear along with their cause, like a dream upon waking up. Even if without beginning, ignorance is not eternal, as in the case of a prior nonexistence. (198-99)

> Ignorance is considered to be "without beginning" (*anādi*), not literally but only because no one can say *when* it began. The "prior nonexistence" (*prāg-abhāva*) also, like ignorance, is considered to be "without beginning." Before a jar is manufactured, it is obviously nonexistent. Who can say when its nonexistence began?

> When we are asleep, the dream world that we see is both beginningless and endless, in the sense that it feels as if it has always existed and will continue to exist. From the waking standpoint, though, the dream does begin and it does end. In the same way, when we are in ignorance (like at this moment!), the waking world feels like it has always existed and will continue to exist. From the standpoint of knowledge though, even the waking world—like the dream world—begins and ends.

अनादेरपि विध्वंस: प्रागभावस्य वीक्षित: ।
यद्बुद्ध्युपाधिसम्बन्धात्परिकल्पितमात्मनि ॥२००
जीवत्वं न ततोऽन्यत्तु स्वरुपेण विलक्षणम् ।
सम्बन्धस्त्वात्मनो बुद्ध्या मिथ्याज्ञानपुर:सर: ॥ २०१

Even if without beginning, prior nonexistence is seen to have an end. There is no jīva identity different from the one superimposed on the Ātman by its imagined association with the intellect. The association of the Ātman with the intellect is the result of false knowledge. (200-201)

The disciple had raised the possibility of the jīva identity appearing in "some other way" (#192). The teacher squashes that idea and states categorically that it is false knowledge which produces the jīva identity.

विनिवृत्तिर्भवेत्तस्य सम्यग्ज्ञानेन नान्यथा ।
ब्रह्मात्मैकत्वविज्ञानं सम्यग्ज्ञानं श्रुतेर्मतम् ॥ २०२

It (that is, the jīva identity) is destroyed by true knowledge, not by any other means. According to the Vedas, experiencing the self and Brahman as identical is true knowledge. (202)

तदात्मानात्मनो: सम्यग्विवेकेनैव सिध्यति ।
ततो विवेक: कर्तव्य: प्रत्यगात्मासदात्मनो: ॥ २०३

That is attained only through discernment between the self and the non-self. Therefore discernment between the inner self and the false self must be practiced. (203)

जलं पंकवदस्पष्टं पंकापाये जलं स्फुटम् ।
यथा भाति तथात्मापि दोषाभावे स्फुटप्रभ: ॥ २०४

Muddy water is unclear. Just as water becomes clear when the mud is removed, the Ātman also shines brightly when its defects are removed. (204)

The basic "defect" is the Ātman's apparent ignorance of its true nature.

असन्निवृत्तौ तु सदात्मन: स्फुटं प्रतीतिरेतस्य भवेत्प्रतीच: ।
ततो निरास: करणीय एवासदात्मन: साध्वहमादिवस्तुन: ॥ २०५

When the unreal is eliminated, the innermost, real self is experienced directly. Therefore the false self, made up of things like the ego, must be completely eliminated. (205)

अतो नायं परात्मा स्याद्विज्ञानमयशब्दभाक् ।
विकारित्वात्-जडत्वाच्च परिच्छिन्नत्वहेतुतः ।
दृश्यत्वाद्-व्यभिचारित्वात्-नानित्यो नित्य इष्यते ॥ २०६

The layer of knowledge is not the supreme self, because it is (1) prone to change, (2) insentient, (3) limited, (4) an object of perception, and (5) liable to become nonexistent. A transient entity cannot be the eternal self. (206)

The layer of bliss (ānandamaya kośa) is now described (#207-209):

आनन्द-प्रतिबिम्ब-चुम्बिततनु-र्वृत्तिस्तमोजृम्भिता
स्यादानन्दमयः प्रियादिगुणकः स्वेष्टार्थलाभोदयः ।
पुण्यस्यानुभवे विभाति कृतिनामानन्दरूपः स्वयं
सर्वो नन्दति यत्र साधु तनुभृन्मात्रः प्रयत्नं विना ॥ २०७

Born of ignorance, the layer of bliss embodies the reflection of the blissful Ātman. It includes enjoyment in diverse forms and arises when desired objects are attained. It manifests brightly when the virtuous experience the fruits of their good deeds and when all living beings experience bliss without any effort. (207)

The phrase, "enjoyment in diverse forms," is a reference to Taittirīya Upaniṣad, 2. 5.

आनन्दमयकोशस्य सुषुप्तौ स्फूर्तिरुत्कटा ।
स्वप्नजागरयोरीषदिष्टसंदर्शनादिना ॥ २०८

The layer of bliss manifests intensely in deep sleep. In waking and dream states, it manifests mildly on occasions such as when something agreeable is seen. (208)

> The layer of bliss is really the layer of the ego as experiencer (*bhoktā*). It manifests as both joy (*sukha*) and sorrow (*duḥkha*) which result from contact with agreeable and disagreeable objects in the waking and dream states. In the absence of any objects in deep sleep, the layer functions independently and "manifests intensely" as unalloyed joy—hence its name, the "layer of bliss."

नैवायमानन्दमय: परात्मा
सोपाधिकत्वात्-प्रकृतेर्विकारात् ।
कार्यत्वहेतो: सुकृतक्रियायां
विकारसंघात-समाहितत्वात् ॥ २०९

This layer of bliss is not the supreme self, because (1) it has a limitation, (2) it is a product of ignorance, (3) it is the result of meritorious deeds, (4) it is lodged within other layers which are (also) products (of ignorance). (209)

> The layer of bliss is "limited" to being the ego as experiencer. A blissful experience results from "meritorious deeds" (*sukṛta-kriyā*), hence the layer is dependent on a cause.

The Self

Apparently hidden under the five layers or the three bodies is the Ātman, the real me, who is pure consciousness (*cit*), nonmaterial (*ajaḍa*) and unchanging (*avikāra*). Because the real me is nonmaterial, I am beyond the laws of matter—hence I am free. Because the real me is unchanging, the six inevitable changes (birth, growth, transformation, decay, disease, and death) affect the body and mind, not me—hence I am immortal. The true nature of the Ātman is described in the following verses.

पञ्चानामपि कोशानां निषेधे युक्तित: श्रुते: ।
तन्निषेधावधि: साक्षी बोधरूपोऽवशिष्यते ॥ २१०

When all the five layers are negated to the utmost, with reasoning based on the Vedas, what remains is the witness, whose nature is consciousness. (210)

योऽयमात्मा स्वयंज्योति: पञ्चकोशविलक्षण: ।
अवस्थात्रयसाक्षी सन्निर्विकारो निरञ्जन: ।
सदानन्द: स विज्ञेय: स्वात्मत्वेन विपश्चिता ॥ २११

This Ātman, who is (1) self-effulgent, (2) distinct from the five layers, (3) the witness of the three states, (4) real, (5) unchanging, (6) without impurity, and (7) eternally blissful, should be known by the discerning to be their own self. (211)

The Ātman is uncontaminated by the "impurity" called ignorance.

॥ शिष्य उवाच ॥

मिथ्यात्वेन निषिद्धेषु कोशेष्वेतेषु पञ्चसु ।

सर्वाभावं विना किञ्चिन्न पश्याम्यत्र हे गुरो ।

विज्ञेयं किमु वस्त्वस्ति स्वात्मनात्रविपश्चिता ॥ २१२

The disciple said:

O teacher! After the five layers are dismissed as appearances
without any reality, I don't see here anything other than total void.
What indeed should the discerning know to be their own self? (212)

॥ श्रीगुरुरुवाच ॥

सत्यमुक्तं त्वया विद्वन्निपुणोऽसि विचारणे ।

अहमादि-विकारास्ते तदभावोऽयमप्यथ ॥ २१३

सर्वे येनानुभूयन्ते यः स्वयं नानुभूयते ।

तमात्मानं वेदितारं विद्धि बुद्ध्या सुसूक्ष्मया ॥ २१४

The teacher said:

O wise one! What you say is true. You are a skillful thinker. With the
help of a refined intellect, you should know the witnessing self, who
itself is not perceived but who perceives everything including
modifications such as egoism as well as their absence. (213)

तत्साक्षिकं भवेत्तद्यद्यद्येनानुभूयते ।

कस्याप्यननुभूतार्थे साक्षित्वं नोपयुज्यते ॥ २१५

Whatever is perceived by a person has that person as its witness. If something is not perceived by anyone at all, it has no witness. (215)

> Emptiness (*śūnya*)—or total void—lacks evidence because it has no witness and hence it is unprovable. The *experience* of emptiness disproves the *existence* of emptiness, because it affirms the presence of a witness.

असौ स्वसाक्षिकोऽभावो यत: स्वेनानुभूयते ।

अत: परं स्वयं साक्षात्प्रत्यगात्मा न चेतर: ॥ २१६

This [total void] has the Ātman as its witness, because it is perceived by the Ātman. Hence the inner self is itself none other than the supreme self. (216)

> The disciple's statement "I don't see here anything other than total void" (#212) implies, "I *do* see total void." The witness here is the Ātman, which alone remains when all the five layers are eliminated. Because of the Ātman's uniqueness, the supposed distinction between the individual self and the supreme self also vanishes.

जाग्रत्स्वप्नसुषुप्तिषु स्फुटतरं योऽसौ समुज्जृम्भते

प्रत्यग्रूपतया सदाहमहमित्यन्त: स्फुरन्नैकधा ।

नानाकार-विकारभाजिन इमान् पश्यन्नहंधीमुखान्

नित्यानन्द-चिदात्मना स्फुरति तं विद्धि स्वमेतं हृदि ॥ २१७

Know this to be your own self—this which (1) shines very clearly on its own in the states of waking, dream and deep sleep, (2) manifests as the constant, innermost and uniform experience of "I," (3) perceives egoism, the intellect and other layers with their diverse forms and modifications, and (4) makes its presence felt in the heart as the eternal, blissful, conscious self. (217)

घटोदके बिम्बितमर्कबिम्बं
आलोक्य मूढो रविमेव मन्यते ।
तथा चिदाभासमुपाधिसंस्थं
भ्रान्त्याहमित्येव जडोऽभिमन्यते ॥ २१८

Noticing the reflection of the sun in a jar of water a fool thinks that it is the sun. In the same way, an ignorant person is deluded into identifying the reflection of consciousness in material entities as one's self. (218)

> The reflection of consciousness in "material entities" such as the intellect, the mind and the body is what makes them *appear* conscious and we are deluded into thinking of them as self.

घटं जलं तद्गतमर्कबिम्बं
विहाय सर्वं दिवि वीक्ष्यतेऽर्कः ।
तटस्थ एतत्त्रितयावभासकः
स्वयंप्रकाशो विदुषा यथा तथा ॥ २१९

Just as ignoring the jar, the water and the sun's reflection in it, the wise person sees the sun who (1) is distinct from them, (2) illumines those three, and (3) is itself self-illumined—the same is the case here. (219)

> In the same way, ignoring the body, the mind, and the reflection of consciousness in them, the wise perceive the Ātman as the self,

who is distinct from them, illumines them all, and is itself self-illumined. This is described in the following two verses.

देहं धियं चित्प्रतिबिम्बमेवं
विसृज्य बुद्धौ निहितं गुहायाम् ।
द्रष्टारमात्मानमखण्डबोधं
सर्वप्रकाशं सदसद्विलक्षणम् ॥ २२०
नित्यं विभुं सर्वगतं सुसूक्ष्मं
अन्तर्बहि:शून्यमनन्यमात्मन: ।
विज्ञाय सम्यङ्-निजरूपमेतत्
पुमान् विपाप्मा विरजो विमृत्यु: ॥ २२१

In the same way, ignoring the body, the mind, and the reflection of consciousness, a person experiences fully the nature of the Ātman to be (1) the witness, (2) the uninterrupted awareness, (3) the light of all, (4) distinct from the manifest and the unmanifest, (5) eternal, (6) infinite, (7) all-pervading, (8) extremely subtle, (9) without anything inside or outside, (10) peerless—and becomes free from demerit, impurity and mortality. (220-21)

> Although the Sanskrit word *pāpa* is often translated as "sin," it really means demerit, or a grievous error, that results in pain and suffering in some form.

विशोक आनन्दघनो विपश्चित्
स्वयं कुतश्चिन्न बिभेति कश्चित् ।
नान्योऽस्ति पन्था: भवबन्धमुक्ते:
विना स्वतत्त्वावगमं मुमुक्षो: ॥ २२२

The Ātman is (1) free from grief, (2) concentrated bliss, (3) all-knowing, and has (4) no fear of anything. One who seeks freedom from the bondage of the world has no way other than acquiring the knowledge of the self. (222)

> It is not enough to have an intellectual understanding of the nature of the Ātman. What is needed is the *experience* of the Ātman *as self*.

The Absolute

Brahman (lit. vast, infinite, all-pervading) is the absolute reality. When associated with an individual, the reality is known as the Ātman. When associated with no one or nothing in particular, the same reality is known as Brahman. The two are one and the same. The nature of Brahman is described in the following verses. These verses examine the meaning of "that" (*tat*) in the Upaniṣadic statement, "You are that" (*tat tvam asi*).

ब्रह्माभिन्नत्वविज्ञानं भवमोक्षस्य कारणम् ।
येनाद्वितीयमानन्दं ब्रह्म सम्पद्यते बुधै: ॥ २२३

The knowledge of not being different from Brahman is the cause of freedom from saṁsāra. It is through this knowledge that the wise attain the nondual, blissful Brahman. (223)

> "The knowledge of not being different from Brahman" is the *experience* that "I am Brahman" (*ahaṁ brahmāsmi*).

ब्रह्मभूतस्तु संसृत्यै विद्वान्नावर्तते पुन: ।
विज्ञातव्यमत: सम्यग्ब्रह्माभिन्नत्वमात्मन: ॥ २२४

The wise person who has become Brahman does not return to saṃsāra. Hence the identity of Ātman and Brahman must be fully realized. (224)

सत्यं ज्ञानमनन्तं ब्रह्म विशुद्धं परं स्वत:सिद्धम् ।
नित्यानन्दैकरसं प्रत्यगभिन्नं निरन्तरं जयति ॥ २२५

Brahman dwells eternally as (1) real, (2) conscious, (3) infinite, (4) absolutely pure, (5) transcendent, (6) self-effulgent, (7) eternally blissful, (8) identical with the indweller. (225)

Brahman alone exists:

सदिदं परमाद्वैतं स्वस्मादन्यस्य वस्तुनोऽभावात् ।
न ह्यन्यदस्ति किञ्चित् सम्यक् परमार्थतत्त्वबोधदशायाम् ॥ २२६

In the state of complete realization of the absolute truth, there is no other entity present. Hence this reality is supreme and nondual, as there is nothing else apart from it. (226)

यदिदं सकलं विश्वं नानारुपं प्रतीतमज्ञानात् ।
तत्सर्वं ब्रह्मैव प्रत्यस्ताशेषभावनादोषम् ॥ २२७

This entire world of varied forms that is perceived through ignorance is nothing but Brahman, who is free from the error of endless imagination. (227)

मृत्कार्यभूतोऽपि मृदो न भिन्न:
कुम्भोऽस्ति सर्वत्र तु मृत्स्वरुपात् ।

न कुम्भरूपं पृथगस्ति कुम्भ:
कुतो मृषा कल्पितनाममात्र: ॥ २२८

A jar made of clay is not different from clay, being essentially nothing but clay. The "jar" is only an imagination, since there is no object called jar which is distinct from the clay. (228)

Neither the form nor the color of the jar is distinct from the form and the color of the clay that constitutes it.

केनापि मृद्भिन्नतया स्वरूपं
घटस्य संदर्शयितुं न शक्यते ।
अतो घट: कल्पित एव मोहात्
मृदेव सत्यं परमार्थभूतम् ॥ २२९

Since no one can show the jar's form to be different from that of the clay, the jar (as a distinct object) is merely imagined through delusion. The clay alone is the abiding reality (in a clay jar). (229)

सद्ब्रह्मकार्यं सकलं सदैव
सन्मात्रमेनतन्न ततोऽन्यदस्ति ।
अस्तीति यो वक्ति न तस्य मोहो
विनिर्गतो निद्रितवत्प्रजल्प: ॥ २३०

Everything that emerges from Brahman, who is real (*sat*), is always real. There is nothing apart from Brahman. Anyone who says that there is (something apart from it) is still under delusion and babbles like one asleep. (230)

Just as a clay jar does not exist apart from the clay that constitutes it, so the universe does not exist apart from the reality that constitutes it.

ब्रह्मैवेदं विश्वमित्येव वाणी

श्रौती ब्रूतेऽथर्ववनिष्ठा वरिष्ठा ।

तस्मादेतद्ब्रह्ममात्रं हि विश्वं

नाधिष्ठानाद्भिन्नताऽऽरोपितस्य ॥ २३१

"This universe is Brahman alone"—such is the supreme declaration of the Atharva-veda. Hence this universe is nothing but Brahman. That which is superimposed has no reality apart from its substratum. (231)

> The statement, "This universe is Brahman alone," is from the Muṇḍaka Upaniṣad (2.2.11), which is a part of the Atharva-veda.

सत्यं यदि स्याज्जगदेतदात्मनो

अनन्तत्त्वहानिर्निगमाप्रमाणता ।

असत्यवादित्वमपीशितुः स्यात्

नैतत्त्रयं साधु हितं महात्मनाम् ॥ २३२

If this universe were real, it would (1) negate the infinitude of the Ātman, (2) invalidate the scriptures, and also (3) make the Lord a liar. The great ones don't consider this to be proper. (232)

> (1) The infinite, by definition, can only be one and it would no longer be infinite if there were anything else present. (2) The Upaniṣads repeatedly emphasize that Brahman or Ātman alone exists and that the universe is an appearance. (3) Sri Krishna's words in the following verse would be false if the universe were real.

ईश्वरो वस्तुतत्त्वज्ञो न चाहं तेष्ववस्थित: ।
न च मत्स्थानि भूतानीत्येवमेव व्यचीक्लृपत् ॥ २३३

The Lord, who knows the nature of what is real, has declared: "I am not in them" and "nor are they in me." (233)

> The reference is to the Gītā (9. 4–5). Brahman is the only reality. There is neither "them" in whom Brahman can be nor "they" who can be in Brahman.

यदि सत्यं भवेद्विश्वं सुषुप्तावुपलभ्यताम् ।
यन्नोपलभ्यते किञ्चिदतोऽसत्स्वप्नवन्मृषा ॥ २३४

If the universe were real, it would be perceived (even) in deep sleep. Since nothing is perceived then, the universe is unreal, being only an appearance like a dream. (234)

> Whatever is real is eternal, and hence always available. A "temporary reality" like dream is only an appearance, not really real.

अत: पृथङ्नास्ति जगत्परात्मन:
पृथक्प्रतीतिस्तु मृषा गुणाहिवत् ।
आरोपितस्यास्ति किमर्थवत्ता
अधिष्ठानमाभाति तथा भ्रमेण ॥ २३५

Therefore the universe is not different from the supreme self. Its distinct identity is only an appearance, like that of a snake seen instead of a rope. Has the superimposed any meaningful existence? It is merely the mistaken perception of the substratum. (235)

When a rope is mistaken for a snake in semidarkness, the snake
has no real existence. The snake is "merely the mistaken
perception" of the rope.

भ्रान्तस्य यद्यद्भ्रमतः प्रतीतं

ब्रह्मैव तत्तद्रजतं हि शुक्तिः ।

इदंतया ब्रह्म सदेव रुप्यते

त्वारोपितं ब्रह्मणि नाममात्रम् ॥ २३६

Everything that the deluded perceives through mistake is nothing
but Brahman, just as the silver is nothing but mother-of-pearl.
Whatever is perceived as "this" is only a name, it is only Brahman
that is real. (236)

When mother-of-pearl is mistakenly perceived as a piece of silver,
the silver has no real existence. It is only a name. What is real is
the mother-of-pearl.

Every object in this universe may have a distinct name, but it is
also possible to refer to every object by a common name, "this"
(*idam*).

अतः परं ब्रह्म सदद्वितीयं

विशुद्धविज्ञानघनं निरञ्जनम् ।

प्रशान्तमाद्यन्तविहीनमक्रियं

निरन्तरानन्दरसस्वरुपम् ॥ २३७

निरस्तमायाकृतसर्वभेदं

नित्यं ध्रुवं निष्कलमप्रमेयम् ।

अरुपमव्यक्तमनाख्यमव्ययं

ज्योतिः स्वयं किञ्चिदिदं चकास्ति ॥ २३८

Whatever appears as "this" is the supreme Brahman, who is (1) real, (2) nondual, (3) embodiment of pure consciousness, (4) without blemish, (5) serene, (6) birthless and deathless, (7) beyond activity, (8) embodiment of absolute bliss, (9) free from all distinctions created by māyā, (10) eternal, (11) unchanging, (12) indivisible, (13) unknowable (as an object), (14) formless, (15) undifferentiated, (16) nameless, (17) immutable, and (18) self-luminous. (237-38)

> The phrase "pure consciousness" means consciousness *itself*, without any object to be conscious of.

ज्ञातृज्ञेयज्ञानशून्यमनन्तं निर्विकल्पकम् ।
केवलाखण्डचिन्मात्रं परं तत्त्वं विदुर्बुधा: ॥ २३९

The enlightened realize the supreme truth to be (1) beyond (the triad of) the knower, the known, and knowledge, (2) infinite, (3) without any differentiation, and (4) of the essence of indivisible consciousness. (239)

> The qualifier "infinite" implies freedom from the finiteness imposed by the presence of time, space and objects.

अहेयमनुपादेयं मनोवाचामगोचरम् ।
अप्रमेयमनाद्यनन्तं ब्रह्म पूर्णं महन्मह: ॥ २४०

Brahman (being one's own self) can neither be cast away nor received. It is (1) beyond the reach of mind and speech, (2) unknowable (as an object), (3) without beginning or end, (4) whole, and (5) the light which illumines everything. (240)

3

"YOU ARE THAT"

After teaching the disciple how to look deeply into the meaning of "me" (*aham*) and "that" (*tat*) in the previous section, the teacher now gives the disciple the supreme teaching, "You are that" (*tat tvam asi*), from the Chāndogya Upaniṣad (6.8.7).

What distinguishes the individual "me" from the transcendent "that" is incidental, not intrinsic. It looks real, but it is only an appearance. The truth is that the two—"me" and "that"—are really one and the same.

Through reflection (*manana*) and meditation (*nididhyāsana*), the disciple's oneness with "that" is experienced as "I am Brahman" (*aham brahmāsmi*).

Analysis of "You are that"

तत्त्वंपदाभ्यामभिधीयमानयो:
ब्रह्मात्मनो: शोधितयोर्यदीत्थम् ।
श्रुत्या तयोस्तत्त्वमसीति सम्यक्
एकत्वमेव प्रतिपाद्यते मुहु: ॥ २४१

The Vedic passage, "You are that" (*tat tvam asi*) repeatedly affirms the identity of Brahman and Ātman—denoted by the terms "that" (*tat*) and "you" (*tvam*)—whose natures have been examined (in the earlier verses). (241)

> The passage appears in the Chāndogya Upaniṣad (6.8.7). The nature of the Ātman (#213-22) and the nature of Brahman (#223-25) were described earlier.

ऐक्यं तयोर्लक्षितयोर्न वाच्ययो:

निगद्यतेऽन्योन्यविरुद्धधर्मिणो: ।

खद्योत-भान्वोरिव राज-भृत्ययो:

कूपाम्बुराश्यो: परमाणु-मेर्वो: ॥ २४२

The identity between the two is affirmed through the implied meanings of the two (terms "that" and "you") and not their literal meanings, which point to mutually opposite qualities such as between (1) the sun and a glowworm, (2) the king and his servant, (3) the ocean and a well, and (4) Mount Meru and an atom. (242)

> In the passage being cited, the literal meaning of "that" is the Lord (*īśvara*) and the literal meaning of "you" is the embodied self (*jīva*). Their implied meanings are Brahman and Ātman, respectively.

तयोर्विरोधोऽयमुपाधिकल्पितो

न वास्तव: कश्चिदुपाधिरेष: ।

ईशस्य माया महदादिकारणं

जीवस्य कार्यं श्रृणु पञ्चकोशम् ॥ २४३

Their mutually opposite qualities are not intrinsic but projected through superimposition. Listen—the superimposition in the case of the Lord is māyā, which is the cause of *mahat* and the rest. In the case of the embodied self, it is the fivefold layers, which are the effects (of māyā). (243)

For "*mahat* and the rest," see #123. For "the fivefold layers," see #149-209.

एतावुपाधी परजीवयोस्तयो:

सम्यङ्निरासे न परो न जीव: ।

राज्यं नरेन्द्रस्य भटस्य खेटक:

तयोरपोहे न भटो न राजा ॥ २४४

When these two superimpositions—of the Lord and of the embodied self—are totally eliminated, there is neither the Lord nor the embodied self. A king's identity is tied to the kingdom and a soldier's to his shield. When they are lost, there is neither the king nor the soldier. (244)

अथात आदेश इति श्रुति: स्वयं

निषेधति ब्रह्मणि कल्पितं द्वयम् ।

श्रुतिप्रमाणानुगृहीतबोधात्

तयोर्निरास: करणीय एव ॥ २४५

In the passage beginning with, "Now then the description," the Vedas themselves reject the duality superimposed on Brahman. The two superimpositions (of māyā and of the fivefold layers) must be eliminated with the support of Vedic knowledge. (245)

The passage is from the Bṛhadāraṇyaka Upaniṣad (2.3.6)—"Now then the description (of Brahman): 'Not this, not this.'" The repetition of "not this" emphasizes the negation of every possible superimposition on Brahman.

नेदं नेदं कल्पितत्वान्न सत्यं
रज्जौ दृष्ट्याालवत्स्वप्नवच्च ।
इत्थं दृश्यं साधुयुक्त्या व्यपोह्य
ज्ञेय: पश्चादेकभावस्तयोर्यः ॥ २४६

Both (māyā and the fivefold layers) are not real, because they are superimposed, like a snake on a rope and like a dream. In this way, eliminating what is perceived with the help of good reasoning, the oneness (of what remains) should be realized. (246)

The distinction between the Lord and the embodied self is created by the superimposition of māyā (on the Lord) and the fivefold layers (on the embodied self). When the superimpositions are eliminated, the distinction disappears. See #244.

ततस्तु तौ लक्षणया सुलक्ष्यौ
तयोरखण्डैकरसत्वसिद्धये ।
नालं जहत्या न तथाऽजहत्या
किन्तूभयार्थैकतयैव भाव्यम् ॥ २४७

In order to realize their absolute identity, the two (the Lord and the embodied self) therefore should be carefully considered through their implied meanings. Neither the method of rejection nor that of retention is helpful. One must use the method that combines the two. (247)

> When the *literal* meaning doesn't make sense, the *implied* meaning usually does. There are three primary methods of arriving at the implied meaning. The method (*lakṣaṇā*) of (1) rejection (*jahat*), (2) retention (*ajahat*), and (3) part-rejection, part-retention (*jahat-ajahat*). See the examples below.
>
> (1) The phrase *gaṅgāyāṁ ghoṣaḥ,* literally means "a village of cowherds *in* the Ganges"—its implied meaning is that the village is *on* the Ganges. To make sense, "in" is rejected and substituted by "on".
>
> (2) The phrase *śveto dhāvati,* literally means "a white is running" —its implied meaning (from the context) is that a white *horse* is running. To make sense, "white" is retained but "horse" is added to it.
>
> (3) See the following verse for the third method—part-rejection and part-retention—of arriving at the correct meaning.

स देवदत्तोऽयमितीह चैकता

विरुद्धधर्मांशमपास्य कथ्यते ।

यथा तथा तत्त्वमसीतिवाक्ये

विरुद्धधर्मानुभयत्र हित्वा ॥ २४८

संलक्ष्य चिन्मात्रतया सदात्मनो:

अखण्डभाव: परिधीयते बुधै: ।

एवं महावाक्यशतेन कथ्यते

ब्रह्मात्मनोरैक्यमखण्डभाव: ॥ २४९

In the statement "This is that Devadatta," the identity (of Devadatta) is affirmed after rejecting the contradictory attributes.

In the same way, in the statement, "You are that," the contradictory attributes are rejected from both (the Lord and the embodied self) and, observing carefully their essence as consciousness (*cit*), the identity of Brahman and Ātman is recognized by the wise. Thus hundreds of scriptural texts declare the absolute oneness of Brahman and Ātman. (248-49)

> In the sentence "This is that Devadatta," *this* person Devadatta seen at *this* place at *this* time is compared with *that* Devadatta seen at *that* other place at *that* other time. After rejecting the differences in the non-intrinsic details of time and place, while retaining the intrinsic identity of the person, *this* Devadatta is recognized to be the same as *that* Devadatta.

> In the statement, "You are that" (*tat tvam asi*), you (*tvam*, the embodied self or *jīva*) with a limited lifespan, knowledge and power is compared with that (*tat*, the Lord or *īśvara*) with infinite lifespan, knowledge and power. After rejecting the differences in the non-intrinsic details of lifespan, knowledge and power, while retaining their intrinsic identities rooted in consciousness (*cit*), the "two" are seen to be one and the same being.

> Every Vedic statement that affirms the oneness of Brahman and Ātman is known as a *mahāvākya*, "profound statement." The usually cited four among these are representative samples from the four Vedas: Ṛg-veda—"Consciousness is Brahman" (*prajñānaṁ brahma*). Yajur-veda—"I am Brahman" (*ahaṁ brahmāsmi*). Sāma-veda—"You are that" (*tat tvam asi*). Atharva-veda—"This Ātman is Brahman" (*ayam ātmā brahma*).

अस्थूलमित्येतदसन्निरस्य
सिद्धं स्वतो व्योमवदप्रतर्क्यम् ।
अतो मृषामात्रमिदं प्रतीतं
जहीहि यत्स्वात्मतया गृहीतम् ।

ब्रह्माहमित्येव विशुद्धबुद्ध्या
विद्धि स्वमात्मानमखण्डबोधम् ॥ २५०

In the light of passages such as "it is not tangible," eliminate the unreal through purified understanding, and know your own self to be Brahman, the self-evident, absolute awareness, who—like space—is beyond dispute. Hence renounce your current identity, which is only an appearance that you have embraced as your own self. (250)

> The passage, "it is not tangible," occurs in the Bṛhadāraṇyaka Upaniṣad (3.8.8). Just as the *extent* of space is beyond dispute, so is one's identity with Brahman.

The teacher now summarizes the advice given by Uddālaka to Śvetaketu in the Chāndogya Upaniṣad:

मृत्कार्यं सकलं घटादि सततं मृन्मात्रमेवाभितः
तद्वत्सज्जनितं सदात्मकमिदं सन्मात्रमेवाखिलम् ।
यस्मान्नास्ति सतः परं किमपि तत्सत्यं स आत्मा स्वयं
तस्मात्त्वमसि प्रशान्तममलं ब्रह्माद्वयं यत्परम् ॥ २५१

All clay products, such as a jar, are always and in every way merely clay. In the same way, all this universe, which is produced from the real (Brahman) is itself real and is nothing but the real. Since there is nothing beyond the real, it alone is real and it is itself the Ātman. Therefore that unchanging, untainted, and transcendent Brahman is you. (251)

> Just as the reality in a clay-jar is the clay—the teacher tells the disciple—the reality in the universe as well as in you is Brahman.

निद्राकल्पितदेशकालविषयज्ञात्रादि सर्वं यथा
मिथ्या तद्वदिहापि जाग्रति जगत्स्वाज्ञानकार्यत्वत: ।
यस्मादेवमिदं शरीरकरणप्राणाहमाद्यप्यसत्
तस्मात्त्वमसि प्रशान्तममलं ब्रह्माद्वयं यत्परम् ॥ २५२

Just as the place, time, content, and the observer imagined in sleep (while dreaming) are all unreal, so is it here even in the waking world, since the world is the effect of the self's ignorance. This body, the senses, the prāṇa, ego, etc. are also unreal. Therefore that unchanging, untainted, and transcendent Brahman is you. (252)

> Just as the dream world is the result of the self's ignorance of its waking identity, the waking world is the result of the self's ignorance of its Brahman identity.

यत्र भ्रान्त्या कल्पितं तद्विवेके
तत्तन्मात्रं नैव तस्माद्विभिन्नम् ।
स्वप्ने नष्टे स्वप्नविश्वं विचित्रं
स्वस्माद्भिन्नं किन्नु दृष्टं प्रबोधे ॥ २५३

That which is superimposed through ignorance is found through discernment to be the substratum itself, not different from it. When the dream is over upon waking, is the diverse dream world viewed as independent of oneself? (253)

> The dream world does not exist independently of the dreamer, just as (in the snake/rope analogy) the snake does not exist independently of the rope.

The teacher now offers the disciple a meditation on Brahman (#254-64):

जाति-नीति-कुल-गोत्र-दूरगं
नाम-रूप-गुण-दोष-वर्जितम् ।
देश-काल-विषयातिवर्ति यद्
ब्रह्म तत्त्वमसि भावयात्मनि ॥ २५४

Contemplate in your heart that you are Brahman, who (1) is beyond caste, creed, family, and lineage, (2) is free from name, form, qualities, and defects, and (3) transcends place, time and sense objects. (254)

यत्परं सकलवागगोचरं
गोचरं विमलबोधचक्षुष: ।
शुद्धचिद्घनमनादि वस्तु यद्
ब्रह्म तत्त्वमसि भावयात्मनि ॥ २५५

Contemplate in your heart that you are Brahman, who is (1) supreme, (2) beyond the reach of all senses, (3) within reach of one with purified understanding, (4) the embodiment of pure awareness, and (5) eternal. (255)

षड्भिरुर्मिभिरयोगि योगिहृद्-
भावितं न करणैर्विभावितम् ।
बुद्ध्यवेद्यमनवद्यमस्ति यद्
ब्रह्म तत्त्वमसि भावयात्मनि ॥ २५६

Contemplate in your heart that you are Brahman, who is (1) untouched by the six waves, (2) contemplated in a yogī's heart, (3) not revealed by the senses, (4) not known by the intellect, and (5) flawlessly perfect. (256)

> The "six waves" are hunger and thirst (located in prāṇa), grief and delusion (located in the mind), decay and death (located in the body).

भ्रान्तिकल्पित-जगत्कलाश्रयं
स्वाश्रयं च सदसद्विलक्षणम् ।
निष्कलं निरुपमानवद्धि यद्
ब्रह्म तत्त्वमसि भावयात्मनि ॥ २५७

Contemplate in your heart that you are Brahman, who is (1) the support of all the parts of the universe imagined through delusion, (2) its own support (needing no other), (3) distinct from the tangible and the intangible, (4) without any parts, and (5) incomparable. (257)

जन्म-वृद्धि-परिणत्यपक्षय-
व्याधि-नाशन-विहीनमव्ययम् ।
विश्वसृष्ट्यवनघातकारणं
ब्रह्म तत्त्वमसि भावयात्मनि ॥ २५८

Contemplate in your heart that you are Brahman, who is (1) free from birth, growth, transformation, decay, disease, and death, (2) immutable, and (3) the cause of the universe's creation, preservation and dissolution. (258)

अस्तभेदमनपास्तलक्षणं
निस्तरङ्गजलराशिनिश्चलम् ।
नित्यमुक्तमविभक्तमूर्तिं यद्
ब्रह्म तत्त्वमसि भावयात्मनि ॥ २५९

Contemplate in your heart that you are Brahman, who is (1) free from all distinctions, (2) of indestructible nature, (3) immovable like an ocean without waves, (4) eternally free, and (5) indivisible. (259)

एकमेव सदनेककारणं
कारणान्तरनिरास्यकारणम् ।
कार्यकारणविलक्षणं स्वयं
ब्रह्म तत्त्वमसि भावयात्मनि ॥ २६०

Contemplate in your heart that you are Brahman, who is (1) only one but the cause of many, (2) the cause that itself needs no other cause, (3) distinct from both cause and effect, and (4) independent. (260)

> Brahman is the "cause" only in a relative sense but not in reality, since the "effect"—this universe—is not really real.

निर्विकल्पकमनल्पमक्षरं
यत्क्षराक्षर-विलक्षणं परम् ।
नित्यमव्ययसुखं निरञ्जनं
ब्रह्म तत्त्वमसि भावयात्मनि ॥ २६१

Contemplate in your heart that you are Brahman, who is (1) without any differentiation, (2) not limited, (3) not perishable, (4) distinct from both perishable and imperishable, (5) supreme, (6) eternal, (7) unending bliss, and (8) pure. (261)

यद्विभाति सदनेकधा भ्रमात्

नाम-रूप-गुण-विक्रियात्मना ।

हेमवत्स्वयमविक्रियं सदा

ब्रह्म तत्त्वमसि भावयात्मनि ॥ २६२

Contemplate in your heart that you are Brahman, who, like gold, (1) although one, still appears due to delusion as many, differentiated by name, form, quality, and change, and (2) is in itself always unchanged. (262)

> Gold (as gold) is one substance but (as ornaments) can appear to be many different objects. Nevertheless, gold itself remains unchanged even in the form of an ornament.

यच्चकास्त्यनपरं परात्परं

प्रत्यगेकरसमात्मलक्षणम् ।

सत्यचित्सुखमनन्तमव्ययं

ब्रह्म तत्त्वमसि भावयात्मनि ॥ २६३

Contemplate in your heart that you are Brahman, who shines as (1) one beyond whom there is nothing, (2) one beyond māyā, (3) the innermost essence, (4) the true self, (5) of the nature of being, consciousness and bliss, (6) infinite, and (7) immutable. (263)

उक्तमर्थमिममात्मनि स्वयं

भावयेत्प्रथितयुक्तिभिर्धिया ।

संशयादिरहितं कराम्बुवत्
तेन तत्त्वनिगमो भविष्यति ॥ २६४

The truth, just described (in the earlier verses), should be contemplated in the heart with the help of right reasoning. It will lead to the realization of the truth, which is free from doubt etc., like water in the palm of one's hand. (264)

> The "right reasoning" is the reasoning based on the insights in the Upaniṣads. The obstacles to the realization include doubt (saṁśaya or asambhāvanā) and contrary thoughts (viparīta-bhāvanā).

> Seeing water in the palm of my hand keeps me free from doubt (*I am not sure of what I see in my hand*) as well as contrary thoughts (*I see a flower, I don't see any water*).

Nonduality in Practice

स्वं बोधमात्रं परिशुद्धतत्त्वं
विज्ञाय संघे नृपवच्च सैन्ये ।
तदात्मनैवात्मनि सर्वदा स्थितो
विलापय ब्रह्मणि विश्वजातम् ॥ २६५

Recognizing the self in the body and mind—like the king in an army—to be only pure awareness, and remaining always absorbed in that awareness, merge this universe in Brahman. (265)

> To "merge this universe in Brahman" means to recognize the universe to be merely an appearance, without any existence independent of Brahman. If all the names (nāma) and forms (rūpa) in the universe are eliminated, Brahman alone remains.

बुद्धौ गुहायां सदसद्विलक्षणं
ब्रह्मास्ति सत्यं परमद्वितीयम् ।
तदात्मना योऽत्र वसेद्गुहायां
पुनर्न तस्याङ्गगुहाप्रवेश: ॥ २६६

Brahman, who is (1) distinct from the gross and the subtle, (2) real, (3) supreme, and (4) without a second, is in the cave of the heart. One who dwells in the cave (of the body) with the awareness of being Brahman, does not enter the cave of the body again. (266)

In other words, such a person becomes free for ever from the repetitive cycle of birth and death.

ज्ञाते वस्तुन्यपि बलवती वासनाऽनादिरेषा
कर्ता भोक्ताप्यहमिति दृढा याऽस्य संसारहेतु: ।
प्रत्यग्दृष्ट्याऽऽत्मनि निवसता सापनेया प्रयत्नात्
मुक्तिं प्राहुस्तदिह मुनयो वासनातानवं यत् ॥ २६७

Even after knowing the Ātman, there remains the strong, sturdy and timeless tendency to think of oneself as the doer and the experiencer, which causes rebirth. Effort should be made to destroy this tendency by remaining continually identified with the Ātman. The dissolution of this tendency is spiritual freedom here and now—so say the wise. (267)

The mind of a person can remain disturbed for sometime by a vividly terrifying dream even after waking up. In the same way, even after knowing the Ātman, the strong impressions in the mind may continue to linger. These should be destroyed by the practice of doing everything with the awareness of being the Ātman.

अहं ममेति यो भावो देहाक्षादावनात्मनि ।
अध्यासोऽयं निरस्तव्यो विदुषा स्वात्मनिष्ठया ॥ २६८

The identification with non-self entities like the body and the senses as "I" and "mine" is due to superimposition (on the Ātman). It must be destroyed by the wise disciple by remaining identified with the Ātman. (268)

ज्ञात्वा स्वं प्रत्यगात्मानं बुद्धितद्वृत्तिसाक्षिणम् ।
सोऽहमित्येव सद्वृत्त्याऽनात्मन्यात्ममतिं जहि ॥ २६९

Knowing one's inner self, who is the witness of the mind and its thought-waves, renounce the identification with the non-self with the help of the thought-wave, "I am that." (269)

If the mind is imagined to be a lake, every thought, feeling and memory is like a wave in that lake. Such a wave is called *vṛtti*. Stilling of these waves, according to Patañjali, leads to concentration (*yoga*). (*Yoga-sutra,* 1.2)

The "that" in "I am that" (*so'ham*) is the Ātman. The quote is from the Īśa Upaniṣad, 16.

लोकानुवर्तनं त्यक्त्वा त्यक्त्वा देहानुवर्तनम् ।
शास्त्रानुवर्तनं त्यक्त्वा स्वाध्यासापनयं कुरु ॥ २७०

Eliminate the superimposition on the Ātman after giving up
conforming to societal demands, bodily demands and scriptural
demands. (270)

> Doing what is right and appropriate naturally and out of freedom
> is fine. But conforming (*anuvartanam*) to demands and
> expectations out of a sense of duty strengthens the identification
> with the body and mind ("non-self").

लोकवासनया जन्तो: शास्त्रवासनयापि च ।

देहवासनया ज्ञानं यथावन्नैव जायते ॥ २७१

Right knowledge never arises for those who have desires related to
the society, the body and also the scriptures. (271)

> These include the desires for societal recognition, physical
> wellbeing, and scriptural erudition.

संसारकारागृहमोक्षमिच्छो:

अयोमयं पादनिबन्धशृंखलम् ।

वदन्ति तज्ज्ञा: पटु वासनात्रयं

योऽस्माद्विमुक्त: समुपैति मुक्तिम् ॥ २७२

The wise say that these threefold desires (mentioned in the previous
verse) are like the iron chains that bind the feet of one who wants to
be free from the prison of saṁsāra. One who becomes free from
these attains freedom. (272)

जलादिसंसर्गवशात्प्रभूत-
दुर्गन्धिधूताऽगरुदिव्यवासना ।
संघर्षणेनैव विभाति सम्यक्
विधूयमाने सति बाह्यगन्धे ॥ २७३

The sublime fragrance of agarwood bursts forth only when the profoundly bad odor due to its contact with water etc. is removed by friction. (273)

अन्त:श्रितानन्तदुरन्तवासना-
धूलीविलिप्ता परमात्मवासना ।
प्रज्ञातिसंघर्षणतो विशुद्धा
प्रतीयते चन्दनगन्धवत् स्फुटम् ॥ २७४

The desire for the supreme self is covered by the dust of the endless and harmful desires (for the non-self). It manifests clearly, like the fragrance of sandalwood, only when purified by the intense friction of knowledge. (274)

> Agarwood (*aguru*) and sandalwood (*candana*), although different, are used interchangeably in the preceding two verses, as they share the characteristic of producing fragrance through friction.

अनात्मवासनाजालैस्तिरोभूतात्मवासना ।
नित्यात्मनिष्ठया तेषां नाशे भाति स्वयं स्फुटम् ॥ २७५

The desire for the Ātman shines brightly on its own when the innumerable desires for the non-self, which eclipse it, are destroyed by the constant commitment to the Ātman. (275)

यथा यथा प्रत्यगवस्थितं मन:

तथा तथा मुञ्चति बाह्यवासना: ।

नि:शेषमोक्षे सति वासनानां

आत्मानुभूति: प्रतिबन्धशून्या ॥ २७६

The more the mind delves within, the more do the desires for the external world disappear. When the desires are totally eliminated, the experience of the Ātman becomes free from obstacles. (276)

> The experience of the Ātman is not objective (*"This is the Ātman"*) but subjective (*"I am the Ātman"*).

स्वात्मन्येव सदा स्थित्या मनो नश्यति योगिन: ।

वासनानां क्षयश्चात: स्वाध्यासापनयं कुरु ॥ २७७

By continually remaining absorbed in the Ātman, the yogī's mind is destroyed and the desires perish. Therefore get rid of your superimposition. (277)

> The body is destroyed at death, not so the mind, which persists life after life. Only when the mind is destroyed does the apparently cyclical (hence endless) journey through saṃsāra come to an end.

तमो द्वाभ्यां रज: सत्त्वात्सत्त्वं शुद्धेन नश्यति ।

तस्मात्सत्त्वमवष्टभ्य स्वाध्यासापनयं कुरु ॥ २७८

Tamas is destroyed by the other two (*sattva* and *rajas*), *rajas* by *sattva*, and *sattva* by the pure (Ātman). Therefore cultivate *sattva* and get rid of your superimposition. (278)

Sattva is "destroyed" when the superimposition is eliminated and the Ātman shines forth unobstructed.

How is the superimposition eliminated?

प्रारब्धं पुष्यति वपुरिति निश्चित्य निश्चल: ।
धैर्यमालम्ब्य यत्नेन स्वाध्यासापनयं कुरु ॥ २७९

Recognizing that the *prārabdha* karma preserves the body, remain unaffected and, with patience and care, get rid of your superimposition. (279)

> The body dies only when the karma that has begun to yield results (*prārabdha*) is exhausted. Until that happens, it is important to remain unaffected by distractions.

नाहं जीव: परं ब्रह्मेत्यतद्व्यावृत्तिपूर्वकम् ।
वासनावेगत: प्राप्तस्वाध्यासापनयं कुरु ॥ २८०

"I am the supreme Brahman, not an embodied self"—eliminating in this way everything that is non-self, get rid of the superimposition which is caused by the power of desires. (280)

> Desires belong to the mind but feel *as if* they belong to me. In other words, desires are superimposed on the self.

श्रुत्या युक्त्या स्वानुभूत्या ज्ञात्वा सार्वात्म्यमात्मन: ।
क्वचिदाभासत: प्राप्तस्वाध्यासापनयं कुरु ॥ २८१

Knowing the Ātman to be the self of all through (1) the scripture, (2) reason and (3) direct experience, get rid of the superimposition which is caused by reflected consciousness. (281)

> The reflection of consciousness (ābhāsa-caitanya) in body and mind, or in the layers (kośa) over the Ātman, makes them appear conscious. In other words, consciousness is superimposed on the unconscious (jaḍa) elements.

अनादानविसर्गाभ्यामीषन्नास्ति क्रिया मुने: ।
तदेकनिष्ठया नित्यं स्वाध्यासापनयं कुरु ॥ २८२

No activity whatsoever, other than eating food and its elimination, is present in the sage. With constant commitment to the one reality (Brahman), get rid of the superimposition. (282)

> There is no semblance of agency in the sage other than in personal activities like "eating food and its elimination." Everything else happens without any conscious intention (saṅkalpa).

तत्त्वमस्यादिवाक्योत्थब्रह्मात्मैकत्वबोधत: ।
ब्रह्मण्यात्मत्वदाढर्याय स्वाध्यासापनयं कुरु ॥ २८३

The knowledge of the self's identity with Brahman is generated by statements such as "You are that" (tat tvam asi). With that knowledge, get rid of the superimposition, in order to strengthen the identification with Brahman. (283)

अहंभावस्य देहेऽस्मिन्नि:शेषविलयावधि ।
सावधानेन युक्तात्मा स्वाध्यासापनयं कुरु ॥ २८४

Get rid of the superimposition with mindfulness and concentration, until the "I"-sense in this body is totally destroyed. (284)

प्रतीतिर्जीवजगतो: स्वप्नवद्भाति यावता ।
तावन्निरंतरं विद्वन्स्वाध्यासापनयं कुरु ॥ २८५

O wise one, get rid of the superimposition without the least break until the experience of the world and the embodied self becomes like the experience of a dream. (285)

> The person who has woken up realizes that the dream world was not real, so does one who has woken up spiritually realize that neither one's limited identity (as jīva) nor the waking world is real.

निद्राया लोकवार्ताया: शब्दादेरपि विस्मृते: ।
क्वचिन्नावसरं दत्वा चिन्तयात्मानमात्मनि ॥ २८६

Reflect on the (nature of the) Ātman in your mind, without giving any chance for forgetfulness due to sleep, worldly talk and sense objects. (286)

मातापित्रोर्मलोद्भूतं मलमांसमयं वपु: ।
त्यक्त्वा चाण्डालवद्दूरं ब्रह्मीभूय कृती भव ॥ २८७

Cast away—as if it were an outcast—(the identification with) the body of flesh and secretions, which comes into being from the secretions of the mother and the father. Know yourself to be Brahman and become fulfilled. (287)

घटाकाशं महाकाश इवात्मानं परात्मनि ।
विलाप्याखण्डभावेन तूष्णी भव सदा मुने ॥ २८८

O wise one, remain always identified with the state of undivided
reality, merging the (embodied) self with Brahman, like the space in
a jar merging with the space outside it. (288)

> The space in a jar "merges" in the space outside when the jar gets
> out of the way. Similarly, the embodied self "merges" with
> Brahman when the body/mind get out of the way.

स्वप्रकाशमधिष्ठानं स्वयंभूय सदात्मना ।
ब्रह्माण्डमपि पिण्डाण्डं त्यज्यतां मलभाण्डवत् ॥ २८९

Becoming the self-effulgent substratum (Brahman), you—as that
real being—should give up the macrocosm and also the microcosm,
as if they were a receptacle filled with dirt. (289)

> The macrocosm (*brahmāṇḍa*) comprises the entire material
> universe and the microcosm (*piṇḍāṇḍa*) comprises one's own body
> and mind. Like a dirt-filled receptacle, they are of no use. To give
> them up means to stop identifying with the microcosm as "I" and
> the macrocosm as an object of "my" perception.

चिदात्मनि सदानन्दे देहारूढामहंधियम् ।
निवेश्य लिङ्गमुत्सृज्य केवलो भव सर्वदा ॥ २९०

The "I"-sense which is presently located in the body should be
placed in the ever-blissful, conscious Ātman. Remain by yourself
after dis-identifying from the mind. (290)

To dis-identify from the mind means to withdraw the "I"-sense from the mind. Dwelling thus exclusively in one's own self (*kevala* or *svastha*), the person is both nowhere and everywhere at the same time.

यत्रैष जगदाभासो दर्पणान्त: पुरं यथा ।

तद्ब्रह्माहमिति ज्ञात्वा कृतकृत्यो भविष्यसि ॥ २९१

You will attain fulfillment when you know Brahman to be your self, in whom this world appears to exist like the scene inside a mirror. (291)

> To attain fulfillment means to reach a state where everything that needs to be done has been done (*kṛta-kṛtya*). This state is reached through direct experience, not merely through intellectual understanding.

यत्सत्यभूतं निजरूपमाद्यं

चिद्द्वयानन्दमरूपमक्रियम् ।

तदेत्य मिथ्यावपुरुत्सृज-एतत्

शैलूषवद्द्वेषमुपात्तमात्मन: ॥ २९२

Having attained your own real nature, which is (1) conscious, (2) nondual, (3) blissful, (4) without form, (5) beyond activity, and (6) preeminent, remove (the "I"-sense in) this appearance of the body, like an actor who removes the costume (when the play ends). (292)

सर्वात्मना दृश्यमिदं मृषैव

नैवाहमर्थ: क्षणिकत्वदर्शनात् ।

जानाम्यहं सर्वमिति प्रतीति:

कुतोऽहमादे: क्षणिकस्य सिध्येत् ॥ २९३

Whatever is perceived is only an appearance in every way. Observed to be momentary, the "I" too has no real existence. How can the perception "I know everything" be true of "I" and the rest, which are momentary? (293)

> The Ātman, or the true self, who is real and eternal, puts on the cloak of the ego, or the false self, when it seemingly attaches itself to perishable, material entities such as the body, the mind and the senses. Caused by a momentary thought-wave (*vṛtti*) in the mind, every experience of the objective world is transient.

The real "I" is thus clearly different:

अहंपदार्थस्त्वहमादिसाक्षी

नित्यं सुषुप्तावपि भावदर्शनात् ।

ब्रूते ह्यजो नित्य इति श्रुति: स्वयं

तत्प्रत्यगात्मा सदसद्विलक्षण: ॥ २९४

But the real "I," who is the witness of the ego and the rest, is always seen to be present even in deep sleep. The Vedas themselves say: "(The Ātman is) birthless and eternal." Therefore the inner self is different from the gross and the subtle. (294)

> The body is made of gross matter. The mind, the senses and the ego are made of subtle matter. The Ātman, being nonmaterial, is different from them all. The quote: "birthless and eternal" (*ajo nityaḥ*) is from the Kaṭha Upaniṣad (1.2.18).

विकारिणां सर्वविकारवेत्ता

नित्योऽविकारो भवितुं समर्हति ।

मनोरथ-स्वप्न-सुषुप्तिषु स्फुटं
पुन: पुनर्दृष्टमसत्त्वमेतयो: ॥ २९५

One who perceives all the changes in things that change has to be
eternal and unchanging. The unreality of these two (the gross and
the subtle) is repeatedly observed while daydreaming and in dream
and deep sleep. (295)

> Absorbed in daydreaming, a person is no longer conscious of the
> body. The body disappears in dream as well, and both body and
> mind disappear in deep sleep. The contents of our daydream and
> dream, and the "I" attached to them, are transient and unreal.
> Only the unchanging witness "I" is real.

अतोऽभिमानं त्यज मांसपिण्डे
पिण्डाभिमानिन्यपि बुद्धिकल्पिते ।
कालत्रयाबाध्यमखण्डबोधं
ज्ञात्वा स्वमात्मानमुपैहि शान्तिम् ॥ २९६

Therefore stop identifying with this imaginary lump of flesh and the
"I" attached to it. Attain peace, knowing your own self to be the
eternal awareness, unaffected by the past, present and future. (296)

त्यजाभिमानं कुल-गोत्र-नाम-
रुपाश्रमेष्वार्द्रशवाश्रितेषु ।
लिङ्गस्य धर्मानपि कर्तृदादीन्
त्यक्त्वा भवाखण्डसुखस्वरुप: ॥ २९७

Stop identifying with family, lineage, name, form, and the stage of life—all of which relate to the gross body. Be the eternal bliss yourself, after giving up also the characteristics of the subtle body. (297)

> In the text, the word for the gross body is, literally, "moist corpse" (*ārdraśava*), a corpse kept moist through blood and other fluids, and seemingly "alive" due to the light of Ātman's consciousness reflected in it. The characteristics of the subtle body include being a doer (*kartā*) and an experiencer (*bhoktā*).

Most obstacles in the Advaita practice are traceable to the ego:

सन्त्यन्ये प्रतिबन्धाः पुंसः संसारहेतवो दृष्टाः ।
तेषामेवं मूलं प्रथमविकारो भवत्यहंकारः ॥ २९८

There are other obstacles that lead to a person's being in saṁsāra. At their root is egoism (*ahaṁkāra*), which is the first modification (of ignorance). (298)

> The "other obstacles" are desires and the chain-reaction they set up, which includes attachment, anger, grief, delusion, envy, jealousy, and everything else which keep us tied to saṁsāra.

यावत्स्यात्स्वस्य सम्बन्धोऽहंकारेण दुरात्मना ।
तावन्न लेशमात्रापि मुक्तिवार्ता विलक्षणा ॥ २९९

Even the least talk about spiritual liberation, which is unique, is impossible as long as a person is filled with this wretched egoism. (299)

अहंकारग्रहान्मुक्तः स्वरूपमुपपद्यते ।
चन्द्रवद्विमलः पूर्णः सदानन्दः स्वयंप्रभः ॥ ३००

Freed—like the moon—from the clutches of egoism, the person attains the true self, who is pure, infinite, ever blissful, and self-effulgent. (300)

> A mythical view of the solar and lunar eclipses is that the sun and the moon are periodically attacked by a demon named Rāhu and remain in his clutches. The eclipse ends when they are freed. Egoism seems to eclipse the true self in a similar way.

यो वा पुरैषोऽहमिति प्रतीतो
बुद्ध्या प्रक्लृप्तस्तमसाऽतिमूढया ।
तस्यैव निःशेषतया विनाशे
ब्रह्मात्मभावः प्रतिबन्धशून्यः ॥ ३०१

One's identity with Brahman becomes free from obstacles only when there is the total destruction of that which is created by the foolish intellect steeped in ignorance and which is experienced in this body as, "This is me." (301)

> Only when egoism (the "I" attached to the body and mind) is totally destroyed does the "I" identify itself with Brahman.

ब्रह्मानन्दनिधि-र्महाबलवता-ऽहंकारघोराहिना
संवेष्ट्यात्मनि रक्ष्यते गुणमयै-श्चण्डै-स्त्रिभिर्मस्तकैः ।
विज्ञानाख्य-महासिना द्युतिमता विच्छिद्य शीर्ष-त्रयं
निर्मूल्याहिमिमं निधिं सुखकरं धीरोऽनुभोक्तुं क्षमः ॥ ३०२

The bliss of Brahman "treasure" is covered and guarded by an extremely powerful and dreadful egoism "snake" with three fearsome *guṇa* "hoods." The wise person is able to claim this blissful treasure after severing the three hoods and totally decimating the snake with a big and sharpened knowledge "sword." (302)

> The knowledge that kills the egoism "snake" is the direct experience of identity with Brahman.

The "total" decimation of egoism is vital:

यावद्वा यत्किञ्चिद्द्विषदोषस्फूर्तिरस्ति चेद्देहे ।
कथमारोग्याय भवेत्तद्दहन्तापि योगिनो मुक्त्यै ॥ ३०३

So long as the body has even the slightest trace of poison, how can its health be restored? Similar is the effect of egoism on a yogī's spiritual freedom. (303)

> So long as there is even the slightest trace of egoism, there is no possibility of experiencing identity with Brahman and being free.

अहमोऽत्यन्तनिवृत्त्या तत्कृतनानाविकल्पसंहत्या ।
प्रत्यक्तत्त्वविवेकादयमहमस्मीति विन्दते तत्त्वम् ॥ ३०४

One's true nature (as Brahman) is directly experienced when (1) egoism is totally eliminated, (2) all of the diverse identifications it generates are withdrawn, and (3) the inner reality is discerned. (304)

> The identifications generated by egoism were described in #297—family, lineage, name, form, the stage of life (related to the gross body) and being a doer and an experiencer (related to the subtle body).

अहंकारे कर्तर्यहमिति मतिं मुञ्च सहसा
विकारात्मन्यात्मप्रतिफलजुषि स्वस्थितिमुषि ।
यदध्यासात्प्राप्ता जनि-मृति-जरा-दुःखबहुला
प्रतीचश्चिन्मूर्तेस्तव सुखतनोः संसृतिरियम् ॥ ३०५

You—the inner self, conscious and blissful—should give up immediately your identification with the ego, (1) which is prone to change, (2) in whom the Ātman is reflected, and (3) which obscures your true nature. Caused through superimposition, the "I"-sense in the ego leads to this saṁsāra filled with profound misery of birth, decay and death. (305)

सदैकरूपस्य चिदात्मनो विभो:
आनन्दमूर्तेरनवद्यकीर्ते: ।
नैवान्यथा क्वाप्यविकारिणस्ते
विनाहमध्यासममुष्य संसृति: ॥ ३०६

Nothing other than identifying with the ego would have made this relative existence possible for you, who are (1) eternally the same, (2) infinite, (3) blissful, (4) changeless, (5) consciousness, and (6) of untarnished glory. (306)

तस्मादहंकारमिमं स्वशत्रुं
भोक्तुर्गले कण्टकवत्प्रतीतम् ।
विच्छिद्य विज्ञानमहासिना स्फुटं
भुङ्क्ष्वात्मसाम्राज्यसुखं यथेष्टम् ॥ ३०७

Egoism is this enemy which is like a thorn in the throat of one who is eating. Decimating it with the great sword of knowledge, enjoy directly and freely the bliss of dwelling in your own empire. (307)

Dwelling in one's own empire means remaining absorbed in one's true identity as Brahman.

ततोऽहमादेर्विनिवर्त्य वृत्तिं

संत्यक्तराग: परमार्थलाभात् ।

तूष्णीं समास्स्वात्मसुखानुभूत्या

पूर्णात्मना ब्रह्मणि निर्विकल्प: ॥ ३०८

Thereafter you should remain at peace in Brahman, (1) having withdrawn the mind away from egoism etc., (2) being free from attachment because of the highest realization, and (3) enjoying fully the bliss of the Ātman without any distraction. (308)

The "etc." following egoism refers to the diverse identifications generated by egoism. See #297.

समूलकृत्तोऽपि महानहं पुन:

व्युल्लेखित: स्याद्यदि चेतसा क्षणम् ।

संजीव्य विक्षेपशतं करोति

नभस्वता प्रावृषि वारिदो यथा ॥ ३०९

Even after this mighty egoism is rooted out, it can—like a cloud carried by the wind in the rainy season—come to life and create hundreds of distractions if it is allowed (even) for a moment to sprout again in the mind. (309)

Just as the rain-free clouds can "come to life" when the rainy season arrives, so does egoism when it finds a favorable environment in the mind.

निगृह्य शत्रोरहमोऽवकाश:
क्वचिन्न देयो विषयानुचिन्तया ।
स एव संजीवनहेतुरस्य
प्रक्षीणजम्बीरतरोरिवाम्बु ॥ ३१०

Having controlled this enemy, egoism, it should be given no opportunity to think of sense objects, for that alone is what regenerates its life, like water does to an almost dried citron tree. (310)

देहात्मना संस्थित एव कामी
विलक्षण: कामयिता कथं स्यात् ।
अतोऽर्थसन्धानपरत्वमेव
भेदप्रसक्त्या भवबन्धहेतु: ॥ ३११

Only the person who identifies with the body as "me" has desires. How can anyone different have desires? Therefore the pursuit of sense objects alone, by generating duality, becomes the cause of bondage of the world. (311)

> The "bondage of the world" is the bondage created by identifying with material entities such as the body and mind. According to Swami Vivekananda, "the world" is nothing but one's "own body." (CW 4. 244)

134

कार्यप्रवर्धनाद्-बीजप्रवृद्धि: परिदृश्यते ।
कार्यनाशाद्-बीजनाशस्तस्मात्कार्यं निरोधयेत् ॥ ३१२

When the effects burgeon, the seeds are seen to proliferate. When the effects are destroyed, the seeds are destroyed. Therefore the effects must be controlled. (312)

> The cause ("seed") is egoism and its effect is the desire for sense objects. A seed is the cause of the plant and eventually of a tree with flowers and fruits, which generates more seeds. The more the desire for sense objects, the stronger does egoism get.

Even when egoism is apparently rooted out, it may still remain in a subtle form and "come to life" again (#309):

वासनावृद्धित: कार्यं कार्यवृद्ध्या च वासना ।
वर्धते सर्वथा पुंस: संसारो न निवर्तते ॥ ३१३

When the subtle form grows, so does its effect. When the effect grows, so does the subtle form. Thus a person's saṁsāra never comes to an end. (313)

> Just as even a spark is enough to set a clump of dried grass on fire and eventually an entire forest, so is the subtle form of egoism enough to initiate desire for sense objects, which eventually keeps the person revolving in the vicious cycle of saṁsāra.

संसारबन्धविच्छित्यै तद् द्वयं प्रदहेद्यति: ।
वासनावृद्धिरेताभ्यां चिन्तया क्रियया बहि: ॥ ३१४

In order to destroy the bondage of saṁsāra, the self-controlled person should burn those two, because through both thought and external action, the subtle form (of egoism) is strengthened. (314)

"Those two" are the cause and effect described in earlier verses: egoism and the pursuit of sense objects.

Neither the activity of the mind ("thought") nor the activity of the body ("action") is possible without the reflection of consciousness in the body and the mind, which gives rise to the "I"-sense.

ताभ्यां प्रवर्धमाना सा सूते संसृतिमात्मन: ।
त्रयाणां च क्षयोपाय: सर्वावस्थासु सर्वदा ॥ ३१५
सर्वत्र सर्वत: सर्वब्रह्ममात्रावलोकनं ।
सद्भाववासनादाढ्यांत्तित्त्रयं लयमश्नुते ॥ ३१६

When those two grow, the subtle form (of egoism) leads to a person's continuation in saṁsāra. The way to eliminate the three (egoism, thought, and action) is to perceive only Brahman everywhere and in everything, all the time and in every condition. Those three disappear with the strengthening of the desire to be one with Brahman. (315-16)

If one is not able to perceive Brahman in the manner just described, one can try to control the cause by controlling the effect:

क्रियानाशे भवेच्चिन्तानाशोऽस्माद्वासनाक्षय: ।
वासनाप्रक्षयो मोक्ष: सा जीवन्मुक्तिरिष्यते ॥ ३१७

When the action stops, the thinking stops, which leads to the elimination of the subtle form (of egoism). The complete elimination of egoism is freedom. It is known as the state of living in freedom. (317)

The "freedom" described here is the cessation of all bondages, gross and subtle, and absorption in one's own true nature which is eternal, nondual and blissful.

सद्वासनास्फूर्तिविजृम्भणे सति
ह्यसौ विलीना त्वहमादिवासना ।
अतिप्रकृष्टाप्यरुणप्रभायां
विलीयते साधु यथा तमिस्रा ॥ ३१८

The subtle form of ego etc. disappears with the clear blossoming of the desire for the absolute reality (Brahman), just as even the most intense darkness disappears by the light of the sun. (318)

The "etc." after ego refers to the body, the senses, and the sense objects.

तमस्तम:कार्यमनर्थजालं
न दृश्यते सत्युदिते दिनेशे ।
तथाऽद्वयानन्दरसानुभूतौ
नैवास्ति बन्धो न च दु:खगन्ध: ॥ ३१९

Neither darkness nor the numerous problems it creates are seen when the sun rises. In the same way, neither bondage nor even a trace of sorrow exists when the nondual bliss is experienced. (319)

दृश्यं प्रतीतं प्रविलापयन्स्वयं
सन्मात्रमानन्दघनं विभावयन् ।

समाहित: सन्बहिरन्तरं वा

कालं नयेथा: सति कर्मबन्धे ॥ ३२०

To counteract the effects of karma, pass the time carefully, dissolving whatever is seen internally and externally, and meditating on the only reality (Brahman), bliss absolute. (320)

> The internal world (seen through the mind) and the external world (seen through the senses) are "dissolved" by viewing them as merely an appearance, a fleeting play of names and forms—while the only reality is the witness, the unchanging substratum on which everything is apparently projected.

The danger of negligence (#321-29):

प्रमादो ब्रह्मनिष्ठायां न कर्तव्य: कदाचन ।

प्रमादो मृत्युरित्याह भगवान्ब्रह्मण: सुत: ॥ ३२१

There should never be any negligence in one's steadfastness to Brahman. Revered (Sanatkumāra, who is) Brahmā's son said that negligence (*pramāda*) is death itself. (321)

> The words of Sanatkumāra occur in the Udyoga Parva of the *Mahābhārata,* in a section known as Sanatsujāta-Saṁvāda.

न प्रमादादनर्थो ऽन्यो ज्ञानिन: स्वस्वरूपत: ।

ततो मोहस्ततोऽहंधीस्ततो बन्धस्ततो व्यथा ॥ ३२२

To a seeker of knowledge, there is no calamity other than being negligent of one's own true self. This leads to forgetfulness, which gives rise to the ego, which creates bondage, which then produces suffering. (322)

विषयाभिमुखं दृष्ट्वा विद्वांसमपि विस्मृति: ।
विक्षेपयति धीदोषैर्योषा जारमिव प्रियम् ॥ ३२३

Seeing even a learned person hankering after sense objects, the seeker is led astray by the mind's weaknesses, the way a lover is by a woman. (323)

यथापकृष्टं शैवालं क्षणमात्रं न तिष्ठति ।
आवृणोति तथा माया प्राज्ञं वापि पराङ्मुखम् ॥ ३२४

Just as pond scum, when moved aside, does not stay away even for a moment (but covers the water again), māyā covers even a wise person who hankers after sense objects. (324)

> While intellectual understanding may seem to move aside the "pond scum" of worldliness for a moment, the hankering for sense objects just as quickly "covers" the person with worldliness.

लक्ष्यच्युतं चेद्यदि चित्तमीषद्
बहिर्मुखं सन्निपतेत्ततस्तत: ।
प्रमादत: प्रच्युतकेलिकन्दुक:
सोपानपङ्क्तौ पतितो यथा तथा ॥ ३२५

If the mind deviates even a little from the goal due to external hankerings, it keeps falling down, just as a ball negligently dropped on the stairs goes down the steps. (325)

If the mind strays from Brahman, it "keeps falling down" and the seeker becomes identified again with the ego, the mind, the senses, and the body.

विषयेष्वाविशच्चेत: संकल्पयति तद्गुणान् ।

सम्यक्संकल्पनात्काम: कामात्पुंस: प्रवर्तनम् ॥ ३२६

When the mind comes in contact with sense objects, it begins to think of them. Through extensive thinking arises desire, and desire goads the person to action. (326)

तत: स्वरूपविभ्रंशो विभ्रष्टस्तु पतत्यध: ।

पतितस्य विना नाशं पुननरिरोह ईक्ष्यते ॥ ३२७

This leads to deviation from one's real nature. One who deviates thus falls. One who is fallen is ruined and is rarely seen to rise again. (327)

Deviation from one's real identity as Ātman leads to a "fall" into false identities related to the mind, senses and the body and, through them, to sense objects. #326–27 are reminiscent of the Gītā (2. 62–63).

संकल्पं वर्जयेत्तस्मात्सर्वानर्थस्य कारणम् ।

अपथ्यानि हि वस्तूनि व्याधिग्रस्तो यथोत्सृजेत् ॥ ३२८

Hence avoid thinking (of sense objects), which is the cause of all problems, just as a sick person avoids unhealthy diet. (328)

अत: प्रमादान्न परोऽस्ति मृत्यु:

विवेकिनो ब्रह्मविद: समाधौ ।

समाहित: सिद्धिमुपैति सम्यक्

समाहितात्मा भव सावधान: ॥ ३२९

For a discerning seeker of Brahman, therefore, there is no worse death than negligence in absorption (in Brahman). One who is totally absorbed attains success. Be attentive and become absorbed (in Brahman). (329)

जीवतो यस्य कैवल्यं विदेहे स च केवल: ।

यत्किञ्चित्पश्यतो भेदं भयं ब्रूते यजु:श्रुति: ॥ ३३०

One who is free from all identifications while living is free from them even after death. The Yajur-Veda says that fear comes to one who perceives even the slightest separation. (330)

> Identifying with anything as "I" makes everything else "not-I"—and the resulting separation between the "I" and the "not-I" is the primary cause of fear and anxiety. The Yajur-Veda passage on fear occurs in the Taittirīya Upaniṣad (2.7).

यदा कदा वापि विपश्चिदेष

ब्रह्मण्यनन्तेऽप्यणुमात्रभेदम् ।

पश्यत्यथामुष्य भयं तदेव

यदीक्षितं भिन्नतया प्रमादात् ॥ ३३१

When a wise person sees even the least separation in the infinite Brahman, whatever is seen as different due to negligence becomes a source of fear. (331)

श्रुतिस्मृतिन्यायशतैर्निषिद्धे
दृश्येऽत्र य: स्वात्ममतिं करोति ।
उपैति दु:खोपरि दु:खजातं
निषिद्धकर्ता स मलिम्लुचो तथा ॥ ३३२

One who identifies as "I" with sense objects, which are dismissed (as not-I) through reasoning and by hundreds of texts, experiences one misery after another, similar to a person with an impure mind who does forbidden acts. (332)

> The "texts" are identified in the verse as *śruti* (Vedas) and *smṛti* (post-Vedic texts).

सत्याभिसन्धानरतो विमुक्तो
महत्त्वमात्मीयमुपैति नित्यम् ।
मिथ्याभिसन्धानरतस्तु नश्येद्
दृष्टं तदेतद्यदचोरचोरयो: ॥ ३३३

One who is engaged in the quest for the real and is free (from ignorance) attains the eternal glory of the Ātman. But one who is engaged in the quest for the unreal is destroyed. This is seen in the story of one who was a thief and the other who was not. (333)

> The "eternal glory of the Ātman" includes the state of a pure, calm, unflappable mind, which is universally adored and respected. The "quest for the unreal" is really the quest for what *seems to be* real but is not, such as the objective world. The "story of one who was a thief and the other who was not" is described in the Chāndogya Upaniṣad (6.16.1-3). Two suspects accused of theft are asked to

touch a red-hot axe: nothing happens to the innocent while the guilty person's hand is burnt. In the same way, one who seeks the real becomes free; one who seeks the unreal "is destroyed."

यतिरसदनुसन्धिं बन्धहेतुं विहाय
स्वयमयमहमस्मीत्यात्मदृष्ट्यैव तिष्ठेत् ।
सुखयति ननु निष्ठा ब्रह्मणि स्वानुभूत्या
हरति परमविद्याकार्यदुःखं प्रतीतम् ॥ ३३४

The spiritual seeker should give up thinking about the unreal, which is the cause of bondage, and dwell in this self-perception: "I am this (Brahman)." Dwelling in identity with Brahman brings bliss through the experience of one's self, and totally destroys suffering, which is the result of ignorance. (334)

बाह्यानुसन्धिः परिवर्धयेत्फलं
दुर्वासनामेव ततस्ततोऽधिकाम् ।
ज्ञात्वा विवेकैः परिहृत्य बाह्यं
स्वात्मानुसन्धिं विदधीत नित्यम् ॥ ३३५

Dwelling on external objects results only in the flourishing of more and more harmful desires. Knowing this, the discerning should abandon the externals and dwell constantly on one's own (true) self. (335)

What makes the desires "harmful" is that they potentially lead to continued suffering not only in this life but, through rebirth, also beyond death.

143

बाह्ये निरुद्धे मनस: प्रसन्नता
मन:प्रसादे परमात्मदर्शनम् ।
तस्मिन्सुदृष्टे भवबन्धनाशो
बहिर्निरोध: पदवी विमुक्ते: ॥ ३३६

When the externals are shut out, the mind becomes tranquil. When the mind is tranquil, the supreme self (*paramātman*) is perceived. When it is perceived properly, the bondage of the world is destroyed. Hence shutting out the external world provides the path to freedom. (336)

> Perceiving the supreme self "properly" means not seeing it as an object but experiencing it as one's own self. The self is "supreme" only in relation to the self that is embodied (*jīva*). The attributes drop off when the one and only self is directly experienced.

क: पण्डित: सन्सदसद्विवेकी
श्रुतिप्रमाण: परमार्थदर्शी ।
जानन्हि कुर्यादसतोऽवलम्बं
स्वपातहेतो: शिशुवन्मुमुक्षु: ॥ ३३७

Which wise person who (1) discerns between the real and the unreal, (2) accepts the authority of the Vedas, (3) remains focused on the supreme truth, (4) longs for spiritual freedom and (5) definitively knows the danger of one's ruin will—like a child— seek the support of the unreal? (337)

> Children can be immature and sometimes do things that are self-destructive.

144

देहादिसंसक्तिमतो न मुक्ति:
मुक्तस्य देहाद्यभिमत्यभाव: ।
सुप्तस्य नो जागरणं न जाग्रत:
स्वप्नस्तयोर्भिन्नगुणाश्रयत्वात् ॥ ३३८

There is no freedom for one who is identified with the body, etc. There is no identification with the body, etc., for one who is free. One who is asleep is not awake and one who is awake is not dreaming: the two are different states. (338)

> Just as the waking state and the sleep state cannot coexist, the identification with the body, etc. (the "et cetera" includes the mind, the ego and the senses) and spiritual freedom (*mukti*) also cannot coexist.

अन्तर्बहि: स्वं स्थिरजङ्गमेषु
ज्ञानात्मनाधारतया विलोक्य ।
त्यक्ताखिलोपाधिरखण्डरूप:
पूर्णात्मना य: स्थित एष मुक्त: ॥ ३३९

The free person is one who, having experienced the self, within and without, as pure awareness which is the support of everything moving and unmoving, is free from all limitations, and dwells as the infinite, absolute self. (339)

सर्वात्मना बन्धविमुक्तिहेतु:
सर्वात्मभावान्न परोऽस्ति कश्चित् ।
दृश्याग्रहे सत्युपपद्यतेऽसौ
सर्वात्मभावोऽस्य सदात्मनिष्ठया ॥ ३४०

Nothing is higher than identifying the self with everything, which is the cause of absolute freedom from bondage. Through steadfastness (*niṣṭhā*) on the eternal Ātman, when the objective world is not seen, the identification with everything is attained. (340)

> All bondage, symbolized by fear, springs from duality. When the self is identified with everything, there is nothing apart from the self.

दृश्यस्याग्रहणं कथं नु घटते देहात्मना तिष्ठतो

बाह्यार्थानुभवप्रसक्तमनसस्तत्तत्क्रियां कुर्वत: ।

संन्यस्ताखिल-धर्म-कर्म-विषयै-र्नित्यात्मनिष्ठापरै:

तत्त्वज्ञै: करणीयमात्मनि सदानन्देच्छुभिर्यत्नत: ॥ ३४१

How can the objective world not be seen by one who is identified with the body, with a mind that is desirous of enjoying external objects, and indulging in activities toward that end? That can be achieved with effort only by one (1) who knows the truth, (2) who has renounced all duties, work and sense objects, (3) who is always steadfast in the awareness of the Ātman, and (4) who longs for the eternal bliss of the Ātman. (341)

The Practice of Samādhi

सार्वात्म्यसिद्धये भिक्षो: कृतश्रवणकर्मण: ।

समाधिं विदधात्येषा शान्तो दान्त इति श्रुति: ॥ ३४२

To experience identity with everything, the Vedic passage starting with "self-controlled, calm" prescribes samādhi to the sage who has gone through the process of hearing. (342)

> "One who knows [Brahman] becomes self-controlled, calm, withdrawn, patient, and concentrated, seeing the Ātman in one's own body and seeing everything as the Ātman." (Bṛhadāraṇyaka Upaniṣad, 4.4.23). The "process of hearing" (śravaṇa) is the learning of the truth from one's teacher.

आरूढशक्तेरहमो विनाश:
कर्तुन्न शक्य: सहसापि पण्डितै: ।
ये निर्विकल्पाख्यसमाधिनिश्चला:
तानन्तराऽनन्तभवा हि वासना: ॥ ३४३

Other than those who have attained calmness through what is called undifferentiated (nirvikalpa) samādhi, not even the wise can suddenly destroy the "I"-sense that has become powerful, since tendencies develop over countless births. (343)

अहंबुद्ध्यैव मोहिन्या योजयित्वाऽऽवृतेर्बलात् ।
विक्षेपशक्ति: पुरुषं विक्षेपयति तद्गुणै: ॥ ३४४

With the help of the veiling power (āvaraṇa śakti), the projecting power (vikṣepa śakti) connects a person with a deluding "I"-sense and produces distraction through its qualities. (344)

> The qualities of the projecting power include its ability to generate desires and the sense of agency.

विक्षेपशक्तिविजयो विषमो विधातुं
नि:शेषमावरणशक्तिनिवृत्यभावे ।
दृग्दृश्ययो: स्फुटपयोजलवद्विभागे
नश्येत्तदावरणमात्मनि च स्वभावात् ।
नि:संशयेन भवति प्रतिबन्धशून्यो
विक्षेपणं नहि तदा यदि चेन्मृषार्थे ॥ ३४५

It is impossible to conquer the projecting power unless the veiling power is completely rooted out. The veil over the Ātman is naturally destroyed when the seer (subject) and the seen (object) are distinguished clearly like milk from water. If the mind thereafter does not oscillate due to unreal objects, the conquest over the projecting power undoubtedly becomes free from obstacles. (345)

सम्यग्विवेक: स्फुटबोधजन्यो
विभज्य दृग्दृश्यपदार्थतत्त्वम् ।
छिनत्ति मायाकृतमोहबन्धं
यस्माद्विमुक्तस्य पुनर्न संसृति: ॥ ३४६

Born of clear perception, right discernment (*viveka*) separates the seer from the seen and breaks the bond of delusion caused by māyā. One who is freed thus is never reborn. (346)

परावरैकत्वविवेकवह्नि:
दहत्यविद्यागहनं ह्यशेषम् ।
किं स्यात्पुन: संसरणस्य बीजं
अद्वैतभावं समुपेयुषोऽस्य ॥ ३४७

This is because the fire of discernment, which is the knowledge of oneness of Brahman and the embodied self, completely burns down the forest of ignorance. What can be the seed for another birth for one who dwells constantly in the nondual experience? (347)

> When the forest is completely consumed, there is no longer any seed left for regeneration.

आवरणस्य निवृत्तिर्भवति हि सम्यक्पदार्थदर्शनत: ।
मिथ्याज्ञानविनाशस्तद्विक्षेपजनितदु:खनिवृत्ति: ॥ ३४८

When the reality is perceived clearly, the veil (that covers it) disappears, followed by the destruction of false knowledge and the end of suffering it causes through projection. (348)

> This is what happens: (1) the veil of ignorance that covers Brahman vanishes, (2) the false knowledge of the self (as mortal and imperfect) is destroyed, and (3) the suffering caused by this false self-knowledge is eliminated.

The process is similar to what happens when a coiled rope is mistaken for a snake in a semi-lit room:

एतत्त्रितयं दृष्टं सम्यग्रज्जुस्वरूपविज्ञानात् ।
तस्माद्वस्तुसतत्त्वं ज्ञातव्यं बन्धविमुक्तये विदुषा ॥ ३४९

These three occur when the reality of the rope is known. In order to be free from bondage, the wise should know the Real as it is. (349)

> The "three" things that occur when the rope is seen clearly: (1) the veil of ignorance over the rope vanishes, (2) the false knowledge of

the snake is destroyed, and (3) the fear and panic caused by the falsely projected snake is eliminated.

अयोऽग्नियोगादिव सत्समन्वयात्
मात्रादिरूपेण विजृम्भते धी: ।
तत्कार्यमेतद्त्रितयं यतो मृषा
दृष्टं भ्रम-स्वप्न-मनोरथेषु ॥ ३५०

Like iron in contact with fire, the Real in contact with the intellect manifests as the knower etc. These three are seen to be unreal in the states of delusion, dream and imagination. (350)

> The glow of red-hot iron belongs to the fire, not to the iron. In the same way, the threefold manifestation—as the knower, knowledge, and the known—belongs to the intellect, not to Brahman. These three are as unreal as the things we see through delusion or in dream or imagination.

ततो विकारा: प्रकृतेरहंमुखा
देहावसाना विषयाश्च सर्वे ।
क्षणेऽन्यथाभाविन एष आत्मा
नोदेति नाप्येति कदापि नान्यथा ॥ ३५१

In the same way, the results of ignorance—from the "I"-sense to the body as well as all objects—are prone to change in a moment. But the Ātman has no beginning, no end, and it never changes. (351)

> All material objects (including the body and the "I"-sense) are unreal too. They *seem* to exist and, upon reflection, when they are known to be mere appearances, they disappear just as quickly.

नित्याद्वयाखण्डचिदेकरूपो

बुद्ध्यादिसाक्षी सदसद्विलक्षण: ।

अहंपद-प्रत्यय-लक्षितार्थ:

प्रत्यक् सदानन्दघन: परात्मा ॥ ३५२

The supreme self is (1) of the nature of consciousness which is eternal, nondual and indivisible, (2) the witness of the intellect and the rest, (3) distinct from matter both gross and subtle, (4) the implied meaning of the term "I", (5) indwelling, and (6) eternally blissful. (352)

> The Ātman is the implied meaning of the term "I" in the statement, "I am Brahman" (*aham brahmāsmi*).

इत्थं विपश्चित्सदसद्विभज्य

निश्चित्य तत्त्वं निजबोधदृष्ट्या ।

ज्ञात्वा स्वमात्मानमखण्डबोधं

तेभ्यो विमुक्त: स्वयमेव शाम्यति ॥ ३५३

In this way, completely freed from them, the wise seeker attains peace after (1) separating the real from the unreal, (2) determining the truth through reflection, (3) experiencing the self as indivisible consciousness. (353)

> The seeker is freed from "them," meaning, the veil of ignorance, false knowledge, and the consequent suffering. See #348.

अज्ञानहृदयग्रन्थेर्निःशेषविलयस्तदा ।

समाधिनाऽविकल्पेन यदाऽद्वैतात्मदर्शनम् ॥ ३५४

151

When the nondual Ātman is experienced in the state of undifferentiated samādhi, the heart's knot of ignorance disappears for ever. (354)

> All differences—such as between the knower, knowledge and the known—vanish in the state of *nirvikalpa* samādhi. The heart's knot (*granthi*) is the apparent joining of consciousness (*cit*) with matter (*jaḍa*). This impossible feat is seemingly achieved through the power of ignorance.

त्वमहमिदमितीयं कल्पना बुद्धिदोषात्

प्रभवति परमात्मन्यद्वये निर्विशेषे ।

प्रविलसति समाधावस्य सर्वो विकल्पो

विलयनमुपगच्छेद्वस्तुतत्त्वावधृत्या ॥ ३५५

Due to the defects in the mind, imaginations such as "you," "I" and "this" seem to arise in the nondual, attribute-free Brahman. When Brahman is realized in samādhi, all imaginations disappear completely due to the knowledge of Brahman's true nature. (355)

शान्तो दान्त: परमुपरत: क्षान्तियुक्त: समाधिं

कुर्वन्नित्यं कलयति यति: स्वस्य सर्वात्मभावम् ।

तेनाविद्या-तिमिर-जनितान्साधु दग्ध्वा विकल्पान्

ब्रह्माकृत्या निवसति सुखं निष्क्रियो निर्विकल्प: ॥ ३५६

Having totally burnt all imaginations generated in the darkness of ignorance, the seeker with a restrained mind and senses, who is deeply indrawn and forbearing, and who practices samādhi and experiences the self in all, dwells blissfully as Brahman, free from activity and the oscillations of the mind. (356)

समाहिता ये प्रविलाप्य बाह्यं
श्रोत्रादि चेत: स्वमहं चिदात्मनि ।
त एव मुक्ता भवपाशबन्धै:
नान्ये तु पारोक्ष्यकथाभिधायिन: ॥ ३५७

They alone are free from the bondage of relative existence who, through samādhi, merge the external objects, the senses such as hearing, the mind, and the "I"-sense into the Ātman, which is pure consciousness—but not others who merely talk of things without experiencing them. (357)

उपाधिभेदात्स्वयमेव भिद्यते
चोपाध्यपोहे स्वयमेव केवल: ।
तस्मादुपाधेर्विलयाय विद्वान्
वसेत्सदाऽकल्पसमाधिनिष्ठया ॥ ३५८

Brahman appears differentiated only because of the diverse superimpositions. When the superimpositions are destroyed, it remains alone by itself. To destroy these superimpositions, the wise should remain devoted to the practice of undifferentiated samādhi. (358)

सति सक्तो नरो याति सद्भावं ह्येकनिष्ठया ।
कीटको भ्रमरं ध्यायन् भ्रमरत्वाय कल्पते ॥ ३५९

Meditating one-pointedly on Brahman, a person becomes Brahman, just as an insect, thinking intensely of a bee, becomes the bee. (359)

> The bee's life cycle begins as an egg which is hatched into a larva. The "insect" larva remains hidden from sight until it emerges as an adult bee. This gave rise to the myth that the "insect" meditates in seclusion on a bee and "becomes" the bee.

क्रियान्तरासक्तिमपास्य कीटको
ध्यायन्नलित्वं ह्यलिभावमृच्छति ।
तथैव योगी परमात्मतत्त्वं
ध्यात्वा समायाति तदेकनिष्ठया ॥ ३६०

Just as the insect, giving up attachment to any activity other than meditating on the bee, attains the identity of a bee—in the same way, a yogī, meditating on Brahman with one-pointed devotion, attains identity with it. (360)

अतीव सूक्ष्मं परमात्मतत्त्वं
न स्थूलदृष्ट्या प्रतिपत्तुमर्हति ।
समाधिनात्यन्तसुसूक्ष्मवृत्या
ज्ञातव्यमार्यैरतिशुद्धबुद्धिभि: ॥ ३६१

The extremely subtle truth of Brahman cannot be grasped through gross perception. It can be known by the noble ones with perfectly pure minds, with the help of extremely subtle perception acquired through samādhi. (361)

यथा सुवर्णं पुटपाकशोधितं
त्यक्त्वा मलं स्वात्मगुणं समृच्छति ।
तथा मन: सत्त्वरजस्तमोमलं
ध्यानेन सन्त्यज्य समेति तत्त्वम् ॥ ३६२

Just as gold is freed from impurities and attains its own luster when subjected to a process in fire, the mind is freed from the impurities of *sattva, rajas* and *tamas,* and attains Brahman through meditation. (362)

Sattva is also an "impurity" which must be transcended after *rajas* and *tamas* are eliminated through *sattva*'s help. To "attain" Brahman is to know oneself to be Brahman. This happens when all the material layers are eliminated through discernment.

निरन्तराभ्यासवशात्तदित्थं
पक्वं मनो ब्रह्मणि लीयते यदा ।
तदा समाधि: स विकल्पवर्जित:
स्वतोऽद्वयानन्दरसानुभावक: ॥ ३६३

Purified thus by continual practice, when the mind merges in Brahman, what results is samādhi without differentiation, which produces the effortless experience of nondual bliss. (363)

When all the contrary ideas (*viparīta-bhāvanā*) are eliminated through practice, the mind is said to be purified.

समाधिनाऽनेन समस्तवासना-
ग्रन्थेर्विनाशोऽखिलकर्मनाश: ।

अन्तर्बहि: सर्वत एव सर्वदा
स्वरूपविस्फूर्तिरयत्नत: स्यात् ॥ ३६४

As a result of this samādhi, the shackles of all desires are
permanently removed, all karma is destroyed and, there is within
and without, everywhere and always, the spontaneous
manifestation of one's true nature. (364)

श्रुते: शतगुणं विद्यान्मननं मननादपि ।
निदिध्यासं लक्षगुणमनन्तं निर्विकल्पकम् ॥ ३६५

Reflection (*manana*) is a hundred times more superior to hearing
(*śravana*). Meditation (*nididhyāsana*) is a hundred thousand times
more superior to reflection. The undifferentiated samādhi is
infinitely more superior than them all. (365)

> The superiority of a practice is measured by the result it produces.
> There is no comparison with the rest when we consider the result
> of *nirvikalpa* samādhi.

निर्विकल्पकसमाधिना स्फुटं
ब्रह्मतत्त्वमवगम्यते ध्रुवम् ।
नान्यथा चलतया मनोगते:
प्रत्ययान्तरविमिश्रितं भवेत् ॥ ३६६

The truth of Brahman is clearly and definitively known through
undifferentiated samādhi, but not by any other means, because the
mind, being unsettled, can get tarnished by other objects. (366)

अत: समाधत्स्व यतेन्द्रिय: सन्
निरन्तरं शान्तमना: प्रतीचि ।
विध्वंसय ध्वान्तमनाद्यविद्यया
कृतं सदेकत्वविलोकनेन ॥ ३६७

Therefore, with controlled senses and a calm mind, always remain immersed in the inner being. Destroy the darkness of the primordial ignorance by experiencing your identity with the Real. (367)

The ignorance is "primordial" (*anādi*, lit. "without beginning") only in the sense that we don't know *when* it began. If it were really without beginning, it would never end.

How do we reduce the useless activities of the mind?

योगस्य प्रथमद्वारं वाङ्निरोधोऽपरिग्रह: ।
निराशा: च निरीहा च नित्यमेकान्तशीलता ॥ ३६८

The first steps in yoga are control of speech, nonacceptance of gifts, living without expectations and desires, and always seeking solitude. (368)

These "first steps" help in eliminating the useless thought-waves (*vṛtti*) in the mind.

एकान्तस्थितिरिन्द्रियोपरमणे हेतुर्दमश्चेतस:
संरोधे करणं शमेन विलयं यायादहंवासना ।
तेनानन्दरसानुभूतिरचला ब्राह्मी सदा योगिन:
तस्माच्चित्तनिरोध एव सततं कार्य: प्रयत्नान्मुने ॥ ३६९

Living in solitude results in the withdrawal of the senses (*dama*), which leads to the control of the mind (*śama*) which, in turn, dissolves the "I"-sense. As a result, the yogī's experience of the bliss of Brahman is constant and stable. Therefore the spiritual seeker should always try to control the mind. (369)

वाचं नियच्छात्मनि तं नियच्छ
बुद्धौ धियं यच्छ च बुद्धिसाक्षिणि ।
तं चापि पूर्णात्मनि निर्विकल्पे
विलाप्य शान्तिं परमां भजस्व ॥ ३७०

Merge the speech in the mind, then merge that in the intellect. Merge the intellect in the witness self, and merging that in the infinite, undifferentiated self, attain supreme peace. (370)

The witness self (*buddhi-sākṣī*, "witness of the intellect") is the implied meaning of "you" (*tvam*) in the statement "You are That" (*tat tvam asi*). The infinite (*pūrṇa*), undifferentiated (*nirvikalpa*) self is Brahman and is the implied meaning of "That" (*tat*).

देहप्राणेन्द्रियमनो-बुद्ध्यादिभिरुपाधिभि:
यैयैवृत्ते: समायोग: तत्तद्भावोऽस्य योगिन: ।
तन्निवृत्त्या मुने: सम्यक् सर्वोपरमणं सुखम्
संदृश्यते सदानन्द-रसानुभव-विप्लव: ॥ ३७१

The yogī's identity reflects every change in identification with limiting forms such as the body, the prāṇa, the senses, the mind, and the intellect. When the identification disappears, the spiritual seeker gets the joy of withdrawing easily from everything and is seen to experience everlasting bliss. (371)

अन्तस्त्यागो बहिस्त्यागो विरक्तस्यैव युज्यते ।
त्यजत्यन्तर्बहि:सङ्गं विरक्तस्तु मुमुक्षया ॥ ३७२

Only a dispassionate person is fit to renounce both internally and externally. Longing for spiritual freedom, a dispassionate person alone gives up internal and external attachments. (372)

बहिस्तु विषयै: सङ्गं तथान्तरहमादिभि: ।
विरक्त एव शक्नोति त्यक्तुं ब्रह्मणि निष्ठित: ॥ ३७३

Only a dispassionate person, grounded in Brahman, is able to renounce the external attachment to objects and the internal attachment to things such as the ego. (373)

वैराग्यबोधौ पुरुषस्य पक्षिवत्
पक्षौ विजानीहि विचक्षण त्वम् ।
विमुक्ति-सौधाग्रलताधिरोहणं
ताभ्यां विना नान्यतरेण सिध्यति ॥ ३७४

O wise one! Know dispassion and discernment to be like the wings of a bird. Without them both, it is not possible to reach the creeper of spiritual freedom atop an edifice with the help of either one. (374)

In this verse, the word *bodha*, lit. "knowledge," refers to the awareness that results from discernment between the self and the non-self.

अत्यन्तवैराग्यवत: समाधि:
समाहितस्यैव दृढप्रबोध: ।
प्रबुद्धतत्त्वस्य हि बन्धमुक्ति:
मुक्तात्मनो नित्यसुखानुभूति: ॥ ३७५

A person with extreme dispassion attains samādhi. Only the one who attains samādhi experiences steady awareness. The one who is awakened to the truth alone becomes free from bondage. The one who is free experiences eternal bliss. (375)

वैराग्यान् परं सुखस्य जनकं पश्यामि वश्यात्मन:
तच्चेच्छुद्धतरात्मबोधसहितं स्वाराज्यसाम्राज्यधुक् ।
एतद्द्वारमजस्रमुक्तियुवतेर्यस्मात्त्वमस्मात्परं
सर्वत्रास्पृहया सदात्मनि सदा प्रज्ञां कुरु श्रेयसे ॥ ३७६

For a person of self-control, I don't see any source of bliss better than dispassion, and if that is accompanied by the highly purifying self-realization, it leads to sovereignty within and without. Since this is the sublime doorway to eternal freedom, for your own good you should continually fix your mind on the eternal self with intense dispassion. (376)

> Sovereignty "within" (*svārājya*, lit. "sovereignty over oneself") implies independence from others, and sovereignty "without" (*sāmrājya*, lit. "sovereignty over others") implies power over others in the relative world.

आशां छिन्द्धि विषोपमेषु विषयष्वेषैव मृत्यो: सृति:
त्यक्त्वा जातिकुलाश्रमेष्वभिमतिं मुञ्चातिदूरात्क्रिया: ।

देहादावसति त्यजात्मधिषणां प्रज्ञां कुरुष्वात्मनि

त्वं द्रष्टास्यमलोऽसि निर्द्वयपरं ब्रह्मासि यद्वस्तुतः ॥ ३७७

Snap off your craving for sense objects, which are like poison, for it
is the pathway to death. Renouncing the pride of caste, family, and
stage of life, throw all rituals far away. Stop thinking of the body and
the rest as "I" and acquire the knowledge of the Ātman, since you
are really the witness, the pure, the nondual supreme Brahman.
(377)

> Broadly speaking, there are four stages of life (āśrama)—as a
> student (brahmacārī), a householder (gṛhastha), a retired person
> (vānaprasthī), and a monastic (sannyāsī).

लक्ष्ये ब्रह्मणि मानसं दृढतरं संस्थाप्य बाह्येन्द्रियं

स्वस्थाने विनिवेश्य निश्चलतनुश्चोपेक्ष्य देहस्थितिम् ।

ब्रह्मात्मैक्यमुपेत्य तन्मयतया चाखण्डवृत्त्याऽनिशं

ब्रह्मानन्दरसं पिबात्मनि मुदा शून्यैः किमन्यैर्भृशम् ॥ ३७८

Remaining indifferent to the condition of the body, restraining the
senses in their respective centers, focusing the mind intensely on
the goal, Brahman, in a steady posture, and attaining oneness with
Brahman, drink the bliss of Brahman joyfully and ceaselessly in
your own self, without a break. What is the use of other things
which are empty? (378)

> The "other things" are the illusory projections of ignorance. They
> are "empty" because they don't yield any rewards; they, in fact,
> lead to suffering.

अनात्मचिन्तनं त्यक्त्वा कश्मलं दु:खकारणम् ।
चिन्तयात्मानमानन्दरूपं यन्मुक्तिकारणम् ॥ ३७९

Give up thinking of the non-self, which is evil and the cause of
suffering, and think of the Ātman, which is blissful and the cause of
freedom. (379)

एष स्वयंज्योतिरशेषसाक्षी
विज्ञानकोशे विलसत्यजस्रम् ।
लक्ष्यं विधायैनमसद्विलक्षणम्
अखण्डवृत्याऽऽत्मतयाऽनुभावय ॥ ३८०

Self-effulgent and the witness of all, this Ātman shines eternally in
the layer of knowledge. Making this (Ātman) which is distinct from
the unreal the goal, exclude all other thoughts, and experience it as
your own self. (380)

एतमच्छिन्नया वृत्त्या प्रत्ययान्तरशून्यया ।
उल्लेखयन्विजानीयात् स्वस्वरूपतया स्फुटम् ॥ ३८१

Know this (Ātman) clearly to be your own nature by contemplating
on it without break and without any other thought. (381)

अत्रात्मत्वं दृढीकुर्वन्नहमादिषु संत्यजन् ।
उदासीनतया तेषु तिष्ठेत्स्फुटघटादिवत् ॥ ३८२

Strengthening your identity with this (Ātman) and giving up the
identity with the ego and the rest, remain indifferent to everything,
as if they were (trivial) things like a cracked jar. (382)

विशुद्धमन्त:करणं स्वरूपे
निवेश्य साक्षिण्यवबोधमात्रे ।
शनै: शनैर्निश्चलतामुपानयन्
पूर्णं स्वमेवानुविलोकयेत्तत: ॥ ३८३

Fixing the purified mind on one's true nature as the witness, which is pure consciousness, and gradually making the mind still, one should experience one's own infinitude. (383)

देहेन्द्रिय-प्राण-मनो-ऽहमादिभि:
स्वाज्ञानक्लृप्तैरखिलैरुपाधिभि: ।
विमुक्तमात्मानमखण्डरूपं
पूर्णं महाकाशमिवावलोकयेत् ॥ ३८४

Experience the Ātman, indivisible and infinite—like the infinite space—free from all limiting features such as the body, the senses, the prāṇa, the mind, and the ego, produced by one's ignorance. (384)

> Just as space, even if seemingly "enclosed" in different objects, always remains infinite, the Ātman also, even if seemingly enclosed inside a body and a mind, always remains infinite and undivided.

घट-कलश-कुसूल-सूचि-मुख्यै:
गगनमुपाधिशतै: विमुक्तमेकम् ।
भवति न विविधं तथैव शुद्धं
परमहमादिविमुक्तमेकमेव ॥ ३८५

Space is one, not diverse, when freed from hundreds of limiting things such as a jar, a pitcher, a grain container, or a needle. In exactly the same way, the pure Brahman is one, when freed from things such as the ego. (385)

ब्रह्मादिस्तम्बपर्यन्ता मृषामात्रा उपाधय: ।
तत: पूर्णं स्वमात्मानं पश्येदेकात्मना स्थितम् ॥ ३८६

All limiting forms ranging from Brahmā to a blade of grass are not real. Hence one's own self should be experienced as infinite and absolute. (386)

> Even the form of Brahmā, the cosmic being who projects the universe, is "limiting" and is a passing appearance in the infinite Ātman.

यत्र भ्रान्त्या कल्पितं तद्विवेके
तत्तन्मात्रं नैव तस्माद्विभिन्नम् ।
भ्रान्तेर्नाशे भाति दृष्टाहितत्त्वं
रज्जुतद्द्विश्वमात्मस्वरूपम् ॥ ३८७

Through delusion what is mistakenly superimposed on a thing is seen through discernment to be the thing itself, not different from it. When the delusion is removed, what was seen as a snake is known to be a rope. In the same way, what is seen as the world is in reality the Ātman. (387)

स्वयं ब्रह्मा स्वयं विष्णु: स्वयमिन्द्र: स्वयं शिव: ।
स्वयं विश्वमिदं सर्वं स्वस्मादन्यन्न किञ्चन ॥ ३८८

The self is Brahmā, the self is Viṣṇu, the self is Indra, and the self is Śiva. This entire world is the self. Nothing exists apart from the self. (388)

> Everything "apart from the self" *appears* to exist the way a snake *appears* to exist instead of a rope in a semi-lit room.

अन्त: स्वयं चापि बहि: स्वयं च

स्वयं पुरस्तात् स्वयमेव पश्चात् ।

स्वयं ह्यावाच्यां स्वयमप्युदीच्यां

तथोपरिष्टात्स्वयमप्यधस्तात् ॥ ३८९

The self is inside and the self is also outside. The self is in front and the self is also behind. The self is in the south and the self is also in the north. The self is above and the self is also below. (389)

तरङ्ग-फेन-भ्रम-बुद्बुदादि

सर्वं स्वरूपेण जलं यथा तथा ।

चिदेव देहाद्यहमन्तमेतत्

सर्वं चिदेवैकरसं विशुद्धम् ॥ ३९०

The wave, the foam, the whirlpool, the bubbles, and so on are all in reality just water. In the same way, consciousness is all this, from the body to egoism. Everything is uniformly pure consciousness. (390)

> Consciousness has no gradation (hence "uniform") and, being the only existence, it is not contaminated (hence "pure") by association with anything else.

सदेवेदं सर्वं जगदवगतं वाङ्मनसयो:
सतोऽन्यन्नास्त्येव प्रकृतिपरसीम्नि स्थितवत: ।
पृथक् किं मृत्स्नाया: कलश-घट-कुम्भाद्यवगतं
वदत्येष भ्रान्तस्त्वमहमिति मायामदिरया ॥ ३९१

This entire world, known through speech and mind, is Brahman
alone. There is nothing besides Brahman for one who dwells beyond
the limits of nature. Are the pitcher, the jug, the jar, etc. distinct
from the clay? Intoxicated by the wine of māyā, the deluded person
makes distinctions such as "you" and "me." (391)

> Speech (*vāk*) here represents all the senses. The "entire world"
> consists of whatever is perceived by the senses and imagined,
> remembered and thought of by the mind. The "one who dwells
> beyond the limits of nature" is the one who is identified with
> Brahman. The "wine of māyā" is ignorance with its intoxicating
> power to hide and to project.

क्रियासमभिहारेण यत्र नान्यदिति श्रुति: ।
ब्रवीति द्वैतराहित्यं मिथ्याध्यासनिवृत्तये ॥ ३९२

In the passage beginning with, "where one sees nothing else," the
Vedas repeatedly affirm the absence of duality in order to eliminate
a false projection. (392)

> The reference is to the passage from the Chāndogya Upaniṣad
> (7.24.1).

आकाशवन्निर्मल-निर्विकल्पं
नि:सीम-नि:स्पन्दन-निर्विकारम् ।

166

अन्तर्बहिःशून्यमनन्यमद्वयं

स्वयं परं ब्रह्म किमस्ति बोध्यम् ॥ ३९३

Brahman is, like space, (1) without impurity, (2) without distinctions, (3) without boundaries, (4) without activity, (5) without change, and (6) without an inside or an outside. Brahman is the self—unique, nondual and supreme. Knowing it, what remains to be known? (393)

वक्तव्यं किमु विद्यतेऽत्र बहुधा ब्रह्मैव जीवः स्वयं

ब्रह्मैतज्जगदापराणु सकलं ब्रह्माद्वितीयं श्रुतेः ।

ब्रह्मैवाहमिति प्रबुद्धमतयः सन्त्यक्तबाह्याः स्फुटं

ब्रह्मीभूय वसन्ति सन्ततचिदानन्दात्मनैव ध्रुवम् ॥ ३९४

What more need be said here? The embodied self is itself Brahman. This entire world, up to the minutest atom, is Brahman. The Vedas declare Brahman to be nondual. Those who have given up external attachments and have the awakened awareness, "I am Brahman," live clearly identified with Brahman as eternal awareness and bliss. (394)

जहि मलमयकोशेऽहंधियोत्थापिताशा

प्रसभमनिलकल्पे लिङ्गदेहेऽपि पश्चात् ।

निगमगदितकीर्तिं नित्यमानन्दमूर्तिं

स्वयमिति परिचीय ब्रह्मरूपेण तिष्ठ ॥ ३९५

First forcibly destroy the expectations that are created by the ego in the filthy gross body, and then do so also in the subtle body, which is invisible like air. Remain as Brahman, whose glory is described in

the scriptures, after directly experiencing it as the embodiment of
eternal bliss. (395)

शवाकारं यावद्भजति मनुजस्तावदशुचि:
परेभ्य: स्यात्क्लेशो जनन-मरण-व्याधि-निलय: ।
यदात्मानं शुद्धं कलयति शिवाकारमचलं
तदा तेभ्यो मुक्तो भवति हि तदाह श्रुतिरपि ॥ ३९६

As long as a person worships the corpse-like body, dwelling in the
abode of birth, death and disease, the person is impure and suffers
pain from others. One verily becomes free from these when one
thinks of oneself as pure, perfect and the essence of what is good.
This is confirmed by the Vedas. (396)

> A person "worships" the body by wrongly identifying with it as "I".
> The body in itself is "corpse-like": it appears conscious because of
> the presence of the Ātman. For confirmation in the Vedas, see for
> instance the Chāndogya Upaniṣad (8.12.1).

स्वात्मन्यारोपिताशेषाभासवस्तुनिरासत: ।
स्वयमेव परं ब्रह्म पूर्णमद्वयमक्रियम् ॥ ३९७

When the innumerable objects apparently superimposed on one's
self are negated, the supreme Brahman remains by itself as infinite,
nondual, and beyond activity. (397)

समाहितायां सति चित्तवृत्तौ
परात्मनि ब्रह्मणि निर्विकल्पे ।

न दृश्यते कश्चिदयं विकल्प:
प्रजल्पमात्र: परिशिष्यते यत: ॥ ३९८

When the thought-wave of the mind is firmly merged in Brahman the absolute, none of this seeming world is perceived. What remains is only talk. (398)

> The perception of duality vanishes for the enlightened, but it remain as a matter of "talk" on the lips of the ignorant. "All modifications are mere names and efforts of speech" (Chāndogya Upaniṣad, 6.1.4).

असत्कल्पो विकल्पोऽयं विश्वमित्येकवस्तुनि ।
निर्विकारे निराकारे निर्विशेषे भिदा कुत: ॥ ३९९

The existence of this world in the one reality (Brahman) is almost unreal. How can there be any diversity in what is changeless, formless and absolute? (399)

> Referring to the world as "almost" unreal (asat-kalpa) is a concession to our present deluded experience of seeing it as real. The world at least appears to be real. A square circle doesn't even appear to be real, so it is "totally" unreal (asat).

द्रष्टृ-दर्शन-दृश्यादि-भावशून्यैकवस्तुनि ।
निर्विकारे निराकारे निर्विशेषे भिदा कुत: ॥ ४००

How can there be any diversity in the one reality, which is changeless, formless, absolute, and devoid of distinctions such as the perceiver, perception and the perceived? (400)

All "distinctions" belong to the world of duality, which is projected by ignorance.

कल्पार्णव इवात्यन्तपरिपूर्णैकवस्तुनि ।
निर्विकारे निराकारे निर्विशेषे भिदा कुत: ॥ ४०१

How can there be any diversity in the one reality, which is changeless, formless, absolute, and perfectly full like the ocean at the time of dissolution? (401)

तेजसीव तमो यत्र प्रलीनं भ्रान्तिकारणम् ।
अद्वितीये परे तत्त्वे निर्विशेषे भिदा कुत: ॥ ४०२

How can there be any diversity in the supreme reality, which is nondual and absolute, and where the cause of delusion is dissolved like darkness in light? (402)

The primary "cause of delusion" is ignorance.

एकात्मके परे तत्त्वे भेदवार्ता कथं वसेत् ।
सुषुप्तौ सुखमात्रायां भेद: केनावलोकित: ॥ ४०३

How can the idea of duality exist in the supreme reality which is unitary? Who has perceived duality in the pure bliss of deep sleep? (403)

Let alone duality, even the "idea" of duality does not exist in the supreme reality.

न ह्यस्ति विश्वं परतत्त्वबोधात्
सदात्मनि ब्रह्मणि निर्विकल्पे ।

कालत्रये नाप्यहिरीक्षितो गुणे

न ह्याम्बुबिंदुर्मृगतृष्णिकायाम् ॥ ४०४

Even before the supreme truth is realized, the world never exists in Brahman, which is real and nondual. Never is a snake seen to exist in a rope nor a drop of water in the mirage. (404)

> The text uses the phrase "the three stages of time" (kālatraya), namely: past, present and future. The idea of "never" is conveyed by saying that in none of these stages does a snake exist in a rope.

मायामात्रमिदं द्वैतमद्वैतं परमार्थतः ।

इति ब्रूते श्रुतिः साक्षात्सुषुप्तावनुभूयते ॥ ४०५

All this duality is only due to māyā. The supreme truth is nonduality —this is what the Vedas say and this can be experienced directly in deep sleep. (405)

> See, for instance, the Kaṭha Upaniṣad (2.2.11), the Bṛhadāraṇyaka Upaniṣad (2.4.14), the Muṇḍaka Upaniṣad (2.2), and the Chāndogya Upaniṣad (6.14).

अनन्यत्वमधिष्ठानादारोप्यस्य निरीक्षितम् ।

पण्डितैः रज्जुसर्पादौ विकल्पो भ्रान्तिजीवनः ॥ ४०६

The wise have observed, in instances such as the rope-snake, that what is superimposed is not different from the substratum. The difference is perceived due to error. (406)

> When a rope is mistaken for a snake, the *real* rope and the *unreal* snake are not objectively two distinct entities.

171

चित्तमूलो विकल्पोऽयं चित्ताभावे न कश्चन ।
अतश्चित्तं समाधेहि प्रत्यग्रूपे परात्मनि ॥ ४०७

This diversity, which is rooted in the mind, doesn't exist when the mind is absent. Therefore focus the mind on the innermost, supreme self. (407)

> The light of knowledge of the supreme self removes the darkness of ignorance, which naturally eliminates the mind.

किमपि सततबोधं केवलानन्दरूपं
निरुपममतिवेलं नित्यमुक्तं निरीहम् ।
निरवधिगगनाभं निष्कलं निर्विकल्पं
हृदि कलयति विद्वान् ब्रह्म पूर्णं समाधौ ॥ ४०८

In samādhi the wise realize in their heart the infinite Brahman, who is something like (1) constant awareness, (2) pure bliss, (3) incomparable, (4) beyond time, (5) ever free, (6) without activity, (7) without limitations, (8) like space, indivisible and absolute. (408)

> What the wise realize is "something" (*kim api*) because Brahman is really indescribable—and every description of it is, at best, an approximation.

प्रकृतिविकृतिशून्यं भावनातीतभावं
समरसमसमानं मानसम्बन्धदूरम् ।
निगमवचनसिद्धं नित्यमस्मत्प्रसिद्धं
हृदि कलयति विद्वान् ब्रह्म पूर्णं समाधौ ॥ ४०९

172

In samādhi the wise realize in their heart the infinite Brahman, who is (1) free from cause and effect, (2) the reality beyond all thought, (3) homogeneous, (4) matchless, (5) beyond all means of knowledge, (6) known from the scripture, and (7) eternally known to us. (409)

> Brahman is "eternally known" to me because Brahman *is* me. Only in and through Brahman do I know anything else.

अजरममरमस्ताभासवस्तुस्वरूपं
स्तिमितसलिलराशिप्रख्यमाख्याविहीनम् ।
शमितगुणविकारं शाश्वतं शान्तमेकं
हृदि कलयति विद्वान् ब्रह्म पूर्णं समाधौ ॥ ४१०

In samādhi the wise realize in their hearts the infinite Brahman, who is (1) unaging, (2) immortal, (3) the reality free from all false projections, (4) unmoving like a still expanse of water, (5) beyond description, (6) beyond qualities and change, (7) eternal, (8) undisturbed, and (9) one. (410)

समाहितान्तःकरणः स्वरूपे
विलोकयात्मानमखण्डवैभवम् ।
विच्छिन्धि बन्धं भवगन्धगन्धितं
यत्नेन पुंस्त्वं सफलीकुरुष्व ॥ ४११

Focusing the mind on your true nature, experience the Ātman in its indivisible infinitude and destroy the bondage strengthened by the desire for saṁsāra. Make an effort to make your human birth worthwhile. (411)

सर्वोपाधिविनिर्मुक्तं सच्चिदानन्दमद्वयम् ।
भावयात्मानमात्मस्थं न भूय: कल्पसेऽध्वने ॥ ४१२

Meditate on the Ātman as (1) entirely free from all limitations, (2) being, consciousness and bliss, (3) nondual, and (4) dwelling in the heart—and you will never again be entangled in saṁsāra. (412)

The Fruits of Nondual Realization

छायेव पुंस: परिदृश्यमानं
आभासरूपेण फलानुभूत्या ।
शरीरमाराच्छववन्निरस्तं
पुनर्न संधत्त इदं महात्मा ॥ ४१३

As a result of experiencing the Ātman, the enlightened person does not again identify with the body, which appears as a human shadow and is cast off to a distance like a corpse. (413)

> To an enlightened person the body is a mere "human shadow," no better than an object which "is cast off to a distance," since the person's identity has shifted from the body to the Ātman.

सततविमलबोधानन्दरूपं समेत्य
त्यज जडमलरूपोपाधिमेतं सुदूरे ।
अथ पुनरपि नैष स्मर्यतां वान्तवस्तु
स्मरणविषयभूतं कल्पते कुत्सनाय ॥ ४१४

174

Being identified with your nature as eternally pure and blissful
awareness, throw far away this impure and inert limitation and
don't ever think of it again, for a vomited thing elicits disgust when
remembered. (414)

> One's identity with the body—the "impure and inert limitation"—
> must be abandoned for ever in order to identify with the Ātman,
> the "eternally pure and blissful awareness."

समूलमेतत्परिदह्य वह्नौ

सदात्मनि ब्रह्मणि निर्विकल्पे ।

तत: स्वयं नित्यविशुद्धबोधा-

नन्दात्मना तिष्ठति विद्वरिष्ठ: ॥ ४१५

Having burnt all this along with its cause in the fire of Brahman, the
eternal and absolute self, the supremely wise person remains as the
Ātman, the eternally pure and blissful awareness. (415)

> All limitations ("all this") such as the body along with ignorance
> ("its cause") vanish (or are "burnt") when a person is identified
> with Brahman.

प्रारब्धसूत्रग्रथितं शरीरं

प्रयातु वा तिष्ठतु गोरिव स्रक् ।

न तत्पुन: पश्यति तत्त्ववेत्ता

आनन्दात्मनि ब्रह्मणि लीनवृत्ति: ॥ ४१६

Like a cow with a garland, the knower of truth whose mind is
merged in the blissful self, Brahman, does not care if the body dies

or continues to live, composed as it is of karma that has begun to yield fruits (*prārabdha*). (416)

> Just as a cow adorned with a garland is indifferent to it, so is the person identified with Brahman indifferent to the body.

अखण्डानन्दमात्मानं विज्ञाय स्वस्वरूपतः ।
किमिच्छन् कस्य वा हेतोर्देहं पुष्णाति तत्त्ववित् ॥ ४१७

Having known the infinitely blissful Ātman as one's own self, desiring what and for whom would the knower of truth care for the body? (417)

संसिद्धस्य फलं त्वेतज्जीवन्मुक्तस्य योगिनः ।
बहिरन्तः सदानन्दरसास्वादनमात्मनि ॥ ४१८

The yogī who has attained perfection and is the jīvanmukta, gets this result—enjoying the infinite bliss in the mind both inside and outside. (418)

> In order to go to heaven, it is necessary to die, but spiritual freedom is possible here and now. Such perfected yogīs are called the jīvanmukta.

वैराग्यस्य फलं बोधो बोधस्योपरतिः फलम् ।
स्वानन्दानुभवाच्छान्तिरेषैवोपरतेः फलम् ।
यद्युत्तरोत्तराभावः पूर्वपूर्वन्तु निष्फलम् ॥ ४१९

Knowledge is the result of detachment. The mind's withdrawal is the result of awareness. The peace that comes from the experience of the bliss of the self is the result of the mind's withdrawal. If the succeeding stages are absent, the preceding ones become futile. (419)

> This is the chain reaction: detachment (*vairāgya*) leads to the clear perception or knowledge (*bodha*), which leads to the mind's withdrawal (*uparati*) from the senses, which leads to experiencing the bliss of the self (*svānanda*), which leads to peace (*śānti*). All of this happens instinctively in sleep but the effects are temporary. When practiced with effort while being wide awake, the results are permanent. The practice at every stage needs to proceed with perseverance until the result is attained. If it does not, it becomes "futile" (*niṣphala*).

निवृत्ति: परमा तृप्तिरानन्दोऽनुपम: स्वत: ।
दृष्टदु:खेष्वनुद्वेगो विद्याया: प्रस्तुतं फलम् ॥ ४२०

This is the result of knowledge (of the self): (1) withdrawal (from the objective world), (2) supreme fulfillment, (3) spontaneous and incomparable bliss, and (4) serenity in the present suffering. (420)

> In the text, the word for "serenity" is imperturbability (*anudvega*).

यत्कृतं भ्रान्तिवेलायां नाना कर्म जुगप्सितम् ।
पश्चान्नरो विवेकेन तत्कथं कर्तुमर्हति ॥ ४२१

How can a person who did many terrible things in a state of delusion do them again later after acquiring discernment? (421)

> Just as a person with discernment refrains from doing terrible things, a person identified with Brahman refrains from doing anything at all, terrible or not. Whatever good such a person "does" is, really speaking, something that "happens" spontaneously

through the instrumentality of the person's body and mind. The ego being absent, there is no sense of agency.

विद्याफलं स्यादसतो निवृत्ति:
प्रवृत्तिरज्ञानफलं तदीक्षितम् ।
तज्ज्ञाज्ञयोर्यन्मृगतृष्णिकादौ
नोचेद्विदां दृष्टफलं किमस्मात् ॥ ४२२

The result of knowledge is withdrawal from the unreal. The result of ignorance is movement toward the unreal. This difference between the knower and the ignorant is seen in instances such as a mirage. If this were not so, what other visible result is obtained by the knower? (422)

> A knower would not proceed toward a mirage in the desert to obtain water, but an ignorant person would. A knower of Brahman is unaffected by the "mirage" of the world, but an ignorant person is attracted towards it.

अज्ञानहृदयग्रन्थेर्विनाशो यद्यशेषत: ।
अनिच्छोर्विषय: किं नु प्रवृत्ते: कारणं स्वत: ॥ ४२३

When the knot of the heart, which is caused by ignorance, is completely destroyed, what can lead to activity for a person who is naturally free from desire? (423)

> The "knot of the heart" is the knot that ties consciousness with matter. While it is impossible for consciousness and matter to be tied, it *appears* possible because of ignorance. Desire is at the root of action. Absent desire, there is no need to do anything.

वासनानुदयो भोग्ये वैराग्यस्य तदावधि: ।
अहंभावोदयाभावो बोधस्य परमावधि: ।
लीनवृत्तेरनुत्पत्तिर्मर्यादोपरतेस्तु सा ॥ ४२४

The pinnacle of dispassion is reached when desire doesn't arise in
the presence of an object of enjoyment. The supreme pinnacle of
knowledge is reached when the I-sense ceases to arise. The pinnacle
of withdrawal is reached when the thought-wave merged (in
Brahman) does not reappear. (424)

ब्रह्माकारतया सदा स्थिततया निर्मुक्तबाह्यार्थधी:
अन्यावेदितभोग्यभोगकलनो निद्रालुवद्बालवत् ।
स्वप्नालोकितलोकवज्जगदिदं पश्यन्क्वचिल्लब्धधी:
आस्ते कश्चिदनन्तपुण्यफलभुग्धन्य: स मान्यो भुवि ॥ ४२५

Rare is the person, blessed and esteemed on earth, and enjoying the
fruits of endless good deeds, who (1) by dwelling always in
Brahman, is totally free from seeing the external objects as real, (2)
like one sleepy or like a child, consumes only the objects offered by
others, and (3) with awareness anchored (in Brahman), sees this
world as similar to the one seen in dreams. (425)

When offered food and water by others, such a person receives it
"like one sleepy or like a child," without any personal initiative and
sense of agency.

स्थितप्रज्ञो यतिरयं य: सदानन्दमश्नुते ।
ब्रह्मण्येव विलीनात्मा निर्विकारो विनिष्क्रिय: ॥ ४२६

The self-controlled person with steady wisdom is one (1) whose mind is merged (in Brahman), (2) who is changeless, (3) who is beyond activity, and (4) who enjoys eternal bliss. (426)

> The characteristics of a person with "steady wisdom" (*sthitaprajña*) described here are similar to those described in the Gītā (2. 55–72).

ब्रह्मात्मनो: शोधितयोरेकभावावगाहिनी ।

निर्विकल्पा च चिन्मात्रा वृत्ति: प्रज्ञेति कथ्यते ।

सुस्थिताऽसौ भवेद्यस्य स्थितप्रज्ञ: स उच्यते ॥ ४२७

The thought-wave which (1) recognizes the oneness of Brahman and Ātman through analysis, (2) is free from duality, and (3) is focused only on consciousness is called wisdom (*prajñā*). One whose wisdom is profoundly steady is called a person of steady wisdom (*sthitaprajña*). (427)

> At first glance, Brahman and Ātman appear to be different. But "through analysis"—meaning, when studied with discernment (*viveka*)—the two are discovered to be one and the same. This analysis was done in #241–64.

The Characteristics of the Jīvanmukta

यस्य स्थिता भवेत्प्रज्ञा यस्यानन्दो निरन्तर: ।

प्रपञ्चो विस्मृतप्राय: स जीवनमुक्त इष्यते ॥ ४२८

The jīvanmukta is one (1) whose wisdom is steady, (2) whose joy is unceasing, and (3) who has almost forgotten the universe. (428)

If the jīvanmukta were to forget the universe completely, it would be impossible to share the wisdom with the students.

लीनधीरपि जागर्ति जाग्रद्धर्मविवर्जित: ।
बोधो निर्वासनो यस्य स जीवनमुक्त इष्यते ॥ ४२९

The jīvanmukta is one (1) who is alert in spite of the mind being merged (in Brahman), (2) who is without the characteristics of one in the waking state, and (3) whose awareness (of sense objects) is free from desire. (429)

> The "characteristics of the one in the waking state" include a body and mind-centered ego. The "awareness of sense objects" has the potential for desire. Both of these are absent in the jīvanmukta.

शान्तसंसारकलन: कलावानपि निष्कल: ।
य: सचित्तोऽपि निश्चित्त: स जीवनमुक्त इष्यते ॥ ४३०

The jīvanmukta is one (1) whose worries about saṁsāra have ceased, (2) who is learned and yet not learned, and (3) who has a mind and is yet without the mind. (430)

> Established in Brahman, the jīvanmukta is learned and yet could be "not learned" from a secular standpoint. Such person has a mind and yet, because it is free from its usual weaknesses, the person is "without the mind" as we know it.

वर्तमानेऽपि देहेऽस्मिञ्छायावदनुवर्तिनि ।
अहन्ता-ममता-ऽभावो जीवनमुक्तस्य लक्षणम् ॥ ४३१

181

The absence of the ideas of "I" and "mine" even in the existing body which follows like a shadow—is a characteristic of the jīvanmukta. (431)

> The body is "like a shadow" to the jīvanmukta (see #413), not real. Hence the absence of "I" and "mine," as if it were somebody else's body.

अतीताननुसन्धानं भविष्यदविचारणम् ।
औदासीन्यमपि प्राप्तं जीवन्मुक्तस्य लक्षणम् ॥ ४३२

Not exploring the past, not thinking about the future, and remaining detached from the present—is a characteristic of the jīvanmukta. (432)

> The jīvanmukta has realized that the past, the present and the future are artificial constructs of the mind. As Swami Vivekananda said, "Time is but the method of our thinking" (CW 8. 22). The Ātman transcends the idea of time.

गुणदोषविशिष्टेऽस्मिन्स्वभावेन विलक्षणे ।
सर्वत्र समदर्शित्वं जीवन्मुक्तस्य लक्षणम् ॥ ४३३

Seeing everything as same in this world, which is filled with naturally diverse elements with their assets and flaws—is a characteristic of the jīvanmukta. (433)

इष्टानिष्टार्थसम्प्राप्तौ समदर्शितयाऽऽत्मनि ।
उभयत्राविकारित्वं जीवन्मुक्तस्य लक्षणम् ॥ ४३४

When favorable or unfavorable things present themselves, remaining unconcerned in either case by viewing them as same—is a characteristic of the jīvanmukta. (434)

Things are "favorable" or "unfavorable" in the eyes of the ignorant, not of the jīvanmukta.

ब्रह्मानन्दरसास्वादासक्तचित्ततया यते: ।
अन्तर्बहिरविज्ञानं जीवन्मुक्तस्य लक्षणम् ॥ ४३५

Remaining oblivious to what is inside or outside, with the mind immersed in tasting the bliss of Brahman—is a characteristic of the jīvanmukta. (435)

The idea of "inside" or "outside" is absent in a nondual experience.

देहेन्द्रियादौ कर्तव्ये ममाहंभाववर्जित: ।
औदासीन्येन यस्तिष्ठेत् स जीवन्मुक्त इष्यते ॥ ४३६

One who is free from the idea of "I" and "mine" with regard to the body, the senses etc., as well as to duties, and lives with detachment, is said to be the jīvanmukta. (436)

The senses "etc." includes the prāṇa, the mind, the intellect, and the ego.

विज्ञात आत्मनो यस्य ब्रह्मभाव: श्रुतेर्बलात् ।
भवबन्धविनिर्मुक्त: स जीवन्मुक्त इष्यते ॥ ४३७

One who has experienced one's nature as Brahman with the help of scriptures and has become totally free from the bondage of saṁsāra is said to be the jīvanmukta. (437)

देहेन्द्रियेष्वहंभाव इदंभावस्तदन्यके ।
यस्य नो भवत: क्वापि स जीवन्मुक्त इष्यते ॥ ४३८

One who never has the idea of "I" with regard to the body and the senses, and the idea of "this" with regard to other things, is said to be the jīvanmukta. (438)

> The body, the senses and "other things" are all material and, as mere superimpositions, identical. The different ways of relating to them—as "I" or "this"—result from past experience.

न प्रत्यग्ब्रह्मणोर्भेदं कदापि ब्रह्मसर्गयो: ।
प्रज्ञया यो विजानाति स जीवन्मुक्त इष्यते ॥ ४३९

One who knows through experience that there is no distinction between the embodied self (jīva) and Brahman, and between Brahman and the world, is said to be the jīvanmukta. (439)

साधुभि: पूज्यमानेऽस्मिन्पीड्यमानेऽपि दुर्जनै: ।
समभावो भवेद्यस्य स जीवन्मुक्त इष्यते ॥ ४४०

One who maintains equanimity when adored by the good and even when troubled by the wicked is said to be the jīvanmukta. (440)

यत्र प्रविष्टा विषया: परेरिता:
नदीप्रवाहा इव वारिराशौ ।

लिनन्ति सन्मात्रतया न विक्रियां
उत्पादयन्त्येष यतिर्विमुक्तः ॥ ४४१

This self-restrained one, who is identified with existence absolute
and in whom whatever is directed by others merges like rivers in the
sea without producing any change, is completely liberated. (441)

> The jīvanmukta is unaffected by others' praise or blame, the way
> the sea is unaffected when rivers merge into it.

विज्ञातब्रह्मतत्त्वस्य यथापूर्वं न संसृतिः ।
अस्ति चेन्न स विज्ञातब्रह्मभावो बहिर्मुखः ॥ ४४२

There is no saṁsāra as before for a person who has experienced the
reality of Brahman. If there is, (it means that) the person has
outgoing tendencies and has not experienced identity with
Brahman. (442)

The influence of past karma which has begun (prārabdha) *to yield fruit:*

प्राचीनवासनावेगादसौ संसरतीति चेत् ।
न सदेकत्वविज्ञानान्मन्दी भवति वासना ॥ ४४३

If it is argued that such a person may still have attachment to sense
objects due to the force of desires accumulated from the enormous
past, the answer is no. The experience of identity with Brahman
weakens all desires. (443)

> Just as the darkness of the night is "weakened" the moment sun
> begins to rise on the horizon, so are the desires of the jīvanmukta.

अत्यन्तकामुकस्यापि वृत्ति: कुण्ठति मातरि ।
तथैव ब्रह्मणि जाते पूर्णानन्दे मनीषिण: ॥ ४४४

Even an extremely lustful man's tendencies are subdued in the
presence of his mother. In a similar way, (all worldly tendencies are
subdued) in the illumined person who is identified with Brahman,
which is bliss absolute. (444)

> Immersed in the infinite bliss of Brahman, the jīvanmukta does
> not hanker after the pale reflection of bliss in the material world.

निदिध्यासनशीलस्य बाह्यप्रत्यय ईक्ष्यते ।
ब्रवीति श्रुतिरेतस्य प्रारब्धं फलदर्शनात् ॥ ४४५

One who is habitually engaged in meditation is seen to have
external awareness. The Vedas declare this to be due to prārabdha
karma and it is confirmed by the results. (445)

> See, for instance, the Chāndogya Upaniṣad (6.14.2)—"[For the
> enlightened], there is delay only so long as there is no liberation
> [from the body], then perfection is reached."

सुखाद्यनुभवो यावत्तावत्प्रारब्धमिष्यते ।
फलोदय: क्रियापूर्वो निष्क्रियो न हि कुत्रचित् ॥ ४४६

Prārabdha is acknowledged as long as happiness etc., are
experienced. Every result of karma requires prior activity. Never
does it occur without activity. (446)

Both happiness and sorrow (hence "et cetera") are experienced by the jīvanmukta due to *prārabdha,* which are fruits of actions done in the past.

अहं ब्रह्मेति विज्ञानात्कल्पकोटिशतार्जितम् ।
सञ्चितं विलयं याति प्रबोधात्स्वप्नकर्मवत् ॥ ४४७

When the identity with Brahman is experienced, the karma accumulated through millions of births is destroyed, like the karma in the dream state upon waking. (447)

यत्कृतं स्वप्नवेलायां पुण्यं वा पापमुल्बणम् ।
सुप्तोत्थितस्य किन्तत्स्यात्स्वर्गाय नरकाय वा ॥ ४४८

Can the actions done in the dream state, no matter how good or bad, lead the person upon waking to heaven or hell? (448)

स्वमसङ्गमुदासीनं परिज्ञाय नभो यथा ।
न श्लिष्यति न यत्किञ्चित्कदाचिद्भाविकर्मभिः ॥ ४४९

Having experienced oneself as detached and indifferent like space, the jīvanmukta is never affected in the least by future karma. (449)

Verses #445–49 show that the jīvanmukta is affected neither by the results of the accumulated (*sañcita*) karma of the past nor by the results of the karma that may be done in the future (*āgāmi*), but merely experiences the results of the karma that led to this birth and have begun to yield fruit (*prārabdha*).

न नभो घटयोगेन सुरागन्धेन लिप्यते ।
तथात्मोपाधियोगेन तद्धर्मैर्नैव लिप्यते ॥ ४५०

Just as the space inside a jar is not affected by the smell of alcohol, so is the Ātman not affected by its limitations and their characteristics. (450)

> The apparent "limitations" of the Ātman include the body and the mind, and their "characteristics," which include birth, growth, transformation, decay, disease, and death.

ज्ञानोदयात्पुरारब्धं कर्मज्ञानान्न नश्यति ।

अदत्वा स्वफलं लक्ष्यमुद्दिश्योत्सृष्टबाणवत् ॥ ४५१

The karma ready to yield results before the onset of knowledge is not destroyed by that knowledge without yielding its fruits, like the arrow shot at its target. (451)

व्याघ्रबुद्ध्या विनिर्मुक्तो बाण: पश्चात्तु गोमतौ ।

न तिष्ठति छिनत्त्येव लक्ष्यं वेगेन निर्भरम् ॥ ४५२

The arrow that is shot at what is believed to be a tiger but later known to be a cow does not stop, but does pierce the target with full force. (452)

> In the same way, the karma that has begun to yield results does not stop even for a jīvanmukta and is exhausted only through experience.

प्रारब्धं बलवत्तरं खलु विदां भोगेन तस्य क्षय:

सम्यग्ज्ञानहुताशनेन विलय: प्राक्संचितागामिनाम् ।

ब्रह्मात्मैक्यमवेक्ष्य तन्मयतया ये सर्वदा संस्थिता:

तेषां तत्त्रितयं नहि क्वचिदपि ब्रह्मैव ते निर्गुणम् ॥ ४५३

188

Prārabdha is indeed more powerful (than knowledge) for knowers of Brahman and is eliminated only through experiencing its results, but the fire of perfect knowledge destroys the karma accumulated earlier (*sañcita*) and the karma that may be done later (*āgāmi*). None of the three karmas ever affect those who experience their oneness with Brahman and always remain absorbed in that identity. They are indeed the absolute Brahman. (453)

> While the experience of Brahman is identical for every illumined person, the intensity of absorption may vary and that may affect the role of karma in their jīvanmukta state. Hence the intensity with which prārabdha is experienced may also vary.

उपाधितादात्म्यविहीनकेवल-
ब्रह्मात्मनैवात्मनि तिष्ठतो मुने: ।
प्रारब्धसद्भावकथा न युक्ता
स्वप्नार्थसंबन्धकथेव जाग्रत: ॥ ४५४

To speak of the presence of prārabdha in the sage who dwells only in the self as Brahman, free from identifying with any limitations, is as inappropriate as saying that the person awakened from sleep is connected with the objects seen in the dream. (454)

न हि प्रबुद्ध: प्रतिभासदेहे
देहोपयोगिन्यपि च प्रपञ्चे ।
करोत्यहन्तां ममतामिदन्तां
किन्तु स्वयं तिष्ठति जागरेण ॥ ४५५

Awakened from sleep, a person does not identify as "I", "mine" or "this" with the dream body and with the dream objects even if they were useful to the body, but stays awake as the (waking) self. (455)

> In the dream state, the dream body is identified as "I" or "mine" and the dream objects are identified as "mine" or "this," just as in the waking state the present body is identified as "I" or "mine" and the objects as "mine" or "this." These identifications remain confined to the respective states.

न तस्य मिथ्यार्थसमर्थनेच्छा

न संग्रहस्तज्जगतोऽपि दृष्ट: ।

तत्रानुवृत्तिर्यदि चेन्मृषार्थे

न निद्रया मुक्त इतीष्यते ध्रुवम् ॥ ४५६

There is neither the desire to validate the unreal objects nor is that (dream) world accepted as real. If there is still clinging to those unreal objects, the person is clearly not free from sleep. (456)

तद्वत्परे ब्रह्मणि वर्तमान:

सदात्मना तिष्ठति नान्यदीक्षते ।

स्मृतिर्यथा स्वप्नविलोकितार्थे

तथा विद: प्राशनमोचनादौ ॥ ४५७

In the same way, one who is absorbed in Brahman remains identified with that eternal reality and sees nothing else. Just as a person has memory of things seen in a dream, the illumined person has memory of actions such as eating and excreting. (457)

This verse answers the question: How can one who "sees nothing else" carry out everyday human actions? Just as we have memory of unreal things seen in a dream even after we wake up, the illumined person has memory of past actions and is able to do them without being propelled by desire.

कर्मणा निर्मितो देह: प्रारब्धं तस्य कल्प्यताम् ।
नानादेरात्मनो युक्तं नैवात्मा कर्मनिर्मित: ॥ ४५८

The body is the result of karma and prārabdha can be imagined with reference to it. It is not right to imagine it with reference to the birthless Ātman. The Ātman is not the result of karma. (458)

अजो नित्य: शाश्वत इति ब्रुते श्रुतिरमोघवाक् ।
तदात्मना तिष्ठतोऽस्य कुत: प्रारब्धकल्पना ॥ ४५९

The Vedas, whose words are infallible, say: "[The Atman is] birthless, eternal, ever-lasting." How can prārabdha be imagined for a person who is one with the Ātman? (459)

The reference is to the Kaṭha Upaniṣad (1.2.18).

प्रारब्धं सिध्यति तदा यदा देहात्मना स्थिति: ।
देहात्मभावो नैवेष्ट: प्रारब्धं त्यज्यतामत: ॥ ४६०

Prārabdha applies when a person identifies with the body. In this case (of a person who is one with the Ātman), identification with the body is not possible. Hence give up the idea of prārabdha. (460)

It is futile to imagine prārabdha karma affecting an illumined person, who no longer identifies with the body and mind.

शरीरस्यापि प्रारब्धकल्पना भ्रान्तिरेव हि ।

अध्यस्तस्य कुत: सत्त्वमसत्त्वस्य कुतो जनि: ।

अजातस्य कुतो नाश: प्रारब्धमसत: कुत: ॥ ४६१

It is indeed an error to apply prārabdha even to the body. How can
something that is superimposed have existence? How can
something that doesn't exist be born? How can something that is
never born be destroyed? How can prārabdha be applied to
something that doesn't exist? (461)

> Existence is inseparable from reality. A thing exists only if it is real.
> The body is superimposed on the Ātman, just as the snake is
> superimposed on a coiled rope. The Ātman is real, the body isn't.
> Everything other than the Ātman is unreal, even if it *appears* to be
> real.

ज्ञानेनाज्ञानकार्यस्य समूलस्य लयो यदि ।

तिष्ठत्ययं कथं देह इति शङ्कावतो जडान् ।

समाधातुं बाह्यदृष्ट्या प्रारब्धं वदति श्रुति: ॥ ४६२

The Vedas speak about prārabdha from a relative standpoint in
order to resolve this doubt of the dull-witted: "How does the body
survive if knowledge destroys all the effects of ignorance along with
the root cause?" (462)

> The doubt is raised not by the person of knowledge (for whom
> nothing other than Brahman exists) but by "the dull-witted" (*jaḍa*)
> who, because of ignorance, continues to experience the world even
> though it has no absolute existence.

न तु देहादिसत्यत्वबोधनाय विपश्चिताम् ।
यतः श्रुतेरभिप्रायः परमार्थैकगोचरः ॥ ४६३

It is not to affirm the reality of the body etc., to the person of
knowledge, since the purpose of the Vedas is to point only to the one
supreme reality. (463)

> The invoking of prārabdha in the Upaniṣads is not an affirmation
> of the body's reality but a concession to the experience of those still
> in the state of ignorance.

Summary

परिपूर्णमनाद्यन्तमप्रमेयमविक्रियम् ।
एकमेवाद्वयं ब्रह्म नेह नानास्ति किञ्चन ॥ ४६४

Infinite, ineffable, changeless, with no beginning and no end,
Brahman is only one and without a second. There is no duality
whatsoever in it. (464)

> Brahman has no spatial limits, hence it is infinite (paripūrṇa); it
> cannot be known as an object, hence it is ineffable (aprameya).
> The statement, "There is no duality whatsoever in it," is from the
> Kaṭha Upaniṣad (2.1.11). It is repeated in the following six verses
> (#465–70).

सद्घनं चिद्घनं नित्यमानन्दघनमक्रियम् ।
एकमेवाद्वयं ब्रह्म नेह नानास्ति किञ्चन ॥ ४६५

Brahman is only one and without a second, whose nature is existence, consciousness and eternal bliss, and in whom there is no activity. There is no duality whatsoever in it. (465)

> In Brahman there is "no activity" such as the creation, sustenance and destruction of the universe.

प्रत्यगेकरसं पूर्णमनन्तं सर्वतोमुखम् ।
एकमेवाद्वयं ब्रह्म नेह नानास्ति किञ्चन ॥ ४६६

Brahman is only one and without a second, who is within all, homogeneous, infinite, limitless, and all-pervading. There is no duality whatsoever in it. (466)

अहेयमनुपादेयमनादेयमनाश्रयम् ।
एकमेवाद्वयं ब्रह्म नेह नानास्ति किञ्चन ॥ ४६७

Brahman is only one and without a second, who can neither be shunned nor taken up nor accepted, and who is without any support. There is no duality whatsoever in it. (467)

> Being the self, Brahman "can neither be shunned nor taken up nor accepted." It doesn't need any "support," for it alone exists and is itself the support of whatever *appears* to exist.

निर्गुणं निष्कलं सूक्ष्मं निर्विकल्पं निरञ्जनम् ।
एकमेवाद्वयं ब्रह्म नेह नानास्ति किञ्चन ॥ ४६८

Brahman is only one and without a second, who is beyond attributes, without parts, subtle, absolute, and stainless. There is no duality whatsoever in it. (468)

अनिरूप्यस्वरूपं यन्मनोवाचामगोचरम् ।
एकमेवाद्वयं ब्रह्म नेह नानास्ति किञ्चन ॥ ४६९

Brahman is only one and without a second, whose nature is incomprehensible, who is beyond the reach of the mind and speech. There is no duality whatsoever in it. (469)

> Brahman is beyond the reach of all the senses, represented here by "speech." It is intellectually "incomprehensible" precisely because it is beyond the reach of the mind and the senses.

सत्समृद्धं स्वत:सिद्धं शुद्धं बुद्धमनीदृशम् ।
एकमेवाद्वयं ब्रह्म नेह नानास्ति किञ्चन ॥ ४७०

Brahman is only one and without a second, who is real, magnificent, self-existent, pure, aware, and incomparable. There is no duality whatsoever in it. (470)

निरस्तरागा विनिरस्तभोगा:
शान्ता: सुदान्ता यतयो महान्त: ।
विज्ञाय तत्त्वं परमेतदन्ते
प्राप्ता: परां निर्वृतिमात्मयोगात् ॥ ४७१

Having experienced this highest reality, these great seekers who (1) have renounced attachments and desire for enjoyment, and (2) are calm with their senses restrained, attain the supreme bliss in the end by uniting with the Ātman. (471)

> When attachments are renounced, the "desire for enjoyment" naturally wanes. The attainment of supreme bliss "in the end" means either (1) after experiencing Brahman or (2) after the exhaustion of prārabdha. This happens by "uniting with the Ātman," which means experiencing in samādhi one's identity with the Ātman.

भवानपीदं परतत्त्वमात्मन:

स्वरूपमानन्दघनं निचाय्य ।

विधूय मोहं स्वमन:प्रकल्पितं

मुक्त: कृतार्थो भवतु प्रबुद्ध: ॥ ४७२

Having experienced Brahman, the embodiment of bliss, which is your true nature, and casting away the delusion conjured by your mind, may the awakened you be free and attain the goal of life. (472)

समाधिना साधुविनिश्चलात्मना

पश्यात्मतत्त्वं स्फुटबोधचक्षुषा ।

नि:संशयं सम्यगवेक्षितश्चेत्

श्रुत: पदार्थो न पुनर्विकल्पते ॥ ४७३

Experience your identity with the Ātman through the clarity of wisdom acquired by the concentrated mind in samādhi. If it is experienced properly and beyond all doubt, the meaning of the words in the Vedas does not create uncertainty again. (473)

The "meaning of the words in the Vedas"—such as in the statement: "You are that" (*tat tvam asi*)—becomes clear and is confirmed through direct experience.

स्वस्याविद्याबन्धसम्बन्धमोक्षात्
सत्यज्ञानानन्दरुपात्मलब्धौ ।
शास्त्रं युक्तिर्देशिकोक्ति: प्रमाणं
चान्त:सिद्धा स्वानुभूति: प्रमाणम् ॥ ४७४

To experience one's identity as the Ātman—whose nature is existence, consciousness and bliss—by freeing oneself from the bondage of false identity caused of ignorance, the proof is provided by scripture, reasoning, and the words of the guru. Another proof is the inner confirmation acquired through one's own experience. (474)

> The authenticity of "one's own experience" (*svānubhūti*) is confirmed when it is in harmony with the proof provided by scripture (*śāstra*), by the words of the guru (*deśika-ukti*), and through reasoning (*yukti*).

बन्धो मोक्षश्च तृप्तिश्च चिन्ताऽऽरोग्यक्षुधादय: ।
स्वेनैव वेद्या यज्ज्ञानं परेषामानुमानिकम् ॥ ४७५

Bondage, freedom, satisfaction, anxiety, health, thirst, and such things can be experienced only by oneself, since others' knowledge of these is inferential. (475)

> The list includes "such things" as hunger and pain, which can be experienced only personally. Others can only make a guess and it may not be accurate.

तटस्थिता बोधयन्ति गुरव: श्रुतयो यथा ।

प्रज्ञयैव तरेद्विद्वानीश्वरानुगृहीतया ॥ ४७६

Teachers and the Vedas teach from the shore. The wise person crosses (the ocean of saṁsāra) only through direct experience and God's grace. (476)

> Vedānta teachings from external sources are like the training to row a boat being given "from the shore" to a student sitting in the boat. These can only lead to indirect (parokṣa) knowledge. The "ocean of saṁsāra" is crossed only through direct experience. The mystery connecting indirect knowledge to direct experience is "God's grace" (īśvara-anugraha).

स्वानुभूत्या स्वयं ज्ञात्वा स्वमात्मानमखण्डितम् ।

संसिद्ध: सुसुखं तिष्ठेन्निर्विकल्पात्मनाऽऽत्मनि ॥ ४७७

Knowing the self as infinite through one's own experience and with a mind free from doubt, the illumined person remains blissfully immersed in the Ātman. (477)

वेदान्तसिद्धान्तनिरुक्तिरेषा

ब्रह्मैव जीव: सकलं जगच्च ।

अखण्डरूपस्थितिरेव मोक्षो

ब्रह्माद्वितीयं श्रुतय: प्रमाणम् ॥ ४७८

This, in a nutshell, is the conclusion of Vedānta: (1) the jīva and the entire world are nothing but Brahman. (2) Dwelling in the state of identification with the infinite is itself liberation (mokṣa). (3)

Brahman is one without a second—this is known from the authority of the Vedas. (478)

> Dwelling "in the state of identification with the infinite" is the same as identifying oneself as Brahman.

इति गुरुवचनाच्छ्रुतिप्रमाणात्
परमवगम्य सतत्त्वमात्मयुक्त्या ।
प्रशमितकरण: समाहितात्मा
क्वचिदचलाकृतिरात्मनिष्ठितोऽभूत् ॥ ४७९

Experiencing the supreme reality through the words of the guru, the authority of the Vedas, and one's own reasoning, the disciple then became perfectly still and absorbed in the Ātman, with senses fully at rest and the mind concentrated. (479)

✳

4

EPILOGUE

किञ्चित्कालं समाधाय परे ब्रह्मणि मानसम् ।
उत्थाय परमानन्दादिदं वचनमब्रवीत् ॥ ४८०

Concentrating the mind for some time on the supreme Brahman, the disciple arose and, with supreme joy, spoke as follows: (480)

The Disciple's Response

बुद्धिर्विनष्टा गलिता प्रवृत्ति:
ब्रह्मात्मनोरेकतयाऽधिगत्या ।
इदं न जानेऽप्यनिदं न जाने
किं वा कियद्वा सुखमस्य पारम् ॥ ४८१

Having experienced oneness with Brahman, the mind has vanished, its activities have melted, I don't know this and I also don't know that. Nor do I know the nature and extent of my bliss. (481)

> The body is destroyed with death. The mind "vanishes" for ever when ignorance is destroyed by the knowledge of Brahman. There is no longer the distinction between "this" (*pratyakṣa*, which is directly perceived by the senses) or "that" (*parokṣa*, which is

beyond the reach of the senses), because the idea of objects (*vastu*) has vanished. "The nature and extent" of this bliss are no longer known, because the idea of space (*deśa*) and time (*kāla*) has vanished.

वाचा वक्तुमशक्यमेव मनसा मन्तुं न वा शक्यते
स्वानन्दामृत-पूरपूरित-परब्रह्माम्बुधे-वैभवम् ।
अम्भोराशि-विशीर्ण-वार्षिक-शिलाभावं भजन्मे मन:
यस्यांशांशलवे विलीनमधुनाऽऽनन्दात्मना निर्वृतम् ॥ ४८२

It's impossible for words to express or for the mind to imagine the majesty of the ocean of the supreme Brahman, which is filled to the brim by the nectar-like bliss of the Ātman. Melted into an infinitesimal part of it, like a hailstone merging into the ocean, my mind is now content in that blissful essence. (482)

क्व गतं केन वा नीतं कुत्र लीनमिदं जगत् ।
अधुनैव मया दृष्टं नास्ति किं महदद्भुतम् ॥ ४८३

Where has this world gone? By whom was it taken away? Where did it disappear? It was seen by me just now and it isn't here anymore? It's a profound miracle! (483)

किं हेयं किमुपादेयं किमन्यत्किं विलक्षणम् ।
अखण्डानन्दपीयूषपूर्णे ब्रह्ममहार्णवे ॥ ४८४

In the vast ocean of Brahman filled with the nectar of absolute bliss, what is to be rejected? What is to be accepted? What is "the other"? What is distinct? (484)

In oneness, there is no "other," distinct or not. Hence, also, nothing to reject or to accept. (484)

न किञ्चिदत्र पश्यामि न शृणोमि न वेद्म्यहम् ।
स्वात्मनैव सदानन्दरूपेणास्मि विलक्षण: ॥ ४८५

I neither see nor hear nor know anything here. I exist only as my own eternally blissful self, distinct (from whatever else might *seem to* exist). (485)

> In my present state ("here"), I am just my own self, nothing more and nothing less.

नमो नमस्ते गुरवे महात्मने
विमुक्तसङ्गाय सदुत्तमाय ।
नित्याद्वयानन्द-रसस्वरूपिणे
भूम्ने सदाऽपार-दयाम्बु-धाम्ने ॥ ४८६

Salutations again and again to you, O noble teacher, who are (1) completely free from attachment, (2) the best among the illumined ones, (3) the essence of the eternal, nondual bliss, (4) the infinite, and (5) the reservoir of everlasting, boundless compassion. (486)

यत्कटाक्ष-शशिसान्द्रचन्द्रिका-
पातधूत-भवतापज-श्रम: ।
प्राप्तवानहमखण्डवैभवा-
नन्दमात्मपदमक्षयं क्षणात् ॥ ४८७

(Salutations to you, O noble teacher,) whose glance—like the cool rays of the moon—has removed all of my exhaustion caused by the suffering in saṁsāra and I have at once attained the absolutely magnificent, infinite and unending bliss of the Ātman. (487)

धन्योऽहं कृतकृत्योऽहं विमुक्तोऽहं भवग्रहात् ।
नित्यानन्दस्वरूपोऽहं पूर्णोऽहं त्वदनुग्रहात् ॥ ४८८

I feel blessed. I have done what needed to be done. I am free from the clutches of saṁsāra. I am the essence of eternal bliss. I am infinite—all through your grace. (488)

असङ्गोऽहमनङ्गोऽहमलिङ्गोऽहमभङ्गुर: ।
प्रशान्तोऽहमनन्तोऽहममलोऽहं चिरन्तन: ॥ ४८९

I am unattached. I have no (gross) body. I have no subtle body. I am imperishable. I am in profound peace. I am infinite. I am taintless. I am eternal. (489)

अकर्ताहमभोक्ताहमविकारोऽहमक्रिय: ।
शुद्धबोधस्वरूपोऽहं केवलोऽहं सदाशिव: ॥ ४९०

I am not the doer. I am not the experiencer. I am changeless. I am beyond activity. I am the essence of pure awareness. I am perfect. I am the eternally auspicious. (490)

द्रष्टु: श्रोतुर्वक्तु: कर्तुर्भोक्तुर्विभिन्न एवाहम् ।
नित्य-निरन्तर-निष्क्रिय-नि:सीमासङ्ग-पूर्णबोधात्मा ॥ ४९१

I am indeed different from the seer, the hearer, the doer, and the experiencer. I am the essence of awareness, eternal, undivided, beyond activity, boundless, unattached, and infinite. (491)

नाहमिदं नाहमदोऽप्युभयोरवभासकं परं शुद्धम् ।
बाह्याभ्यन्तरशून्यं पूर्णं ब्रह्माद्वितीयमेवाहम् ॥ ४९२

I am not this, I am not that—I illumine them both, (for) I am indeed Brahman, nondual, supreme, pure, infinite, and without interior or exterior. (492)

> The idea of something being inside or outside is related to the body, not the Ātman.

निरुपममनादितत्त्वं त्वमहमिदमद इति कल्पनादूरम् ।
नित्यानन्दैकरसं सत्यं ब्रह्माद्वितीयमेवाहम् ॥ ४९३

I am indeed Brahman, who is (1) incomparable, (2) reality without a beginning, (3) beyond the ideas such as "you" or "me" or "this" or "that," (6) the essence of eternal bliss, (7) real, and (8) nondual. (493)

नारायणोऽहं नरकान्तकोऽहं
पुरान्तकोऽहं पुरुषोऽहमीश: ।
अखण्डबोधोऽहमशेषसाक्षी
निरीश्वरोऽहं निरहं च निर्मम: ॥ ४९४

I am Nārāyaṇa, I am the slayer of Naraka, I am the slayer of Purāntaka, I am the Indweller, I am the Ruler. I am the infinite awareness, I am the witness of everything, I have no ruler, I am without the idea of "I" and "mine." (494)

> Viṣṇu is said to have slayed the demon Naraka. Śiva is said to have slayed the demon Purāntaka (also known as Tripura).

सर्वेषु भुतेष्वहमेव संस्थितो
ज्ञानात्मनाऽन्तर्बहिराश्रय: सन् ।
भोक्ता च भोग्यं स्वयमेव सर्वं
यद्यत्पृथग्दृष्टमिदन्तया पुरा ॥ ४९५

I dwell as awareness in all, being their support both internal and external. I am both the experiencer and the experienced—everything that was experienced as a distinct object before. (495)

> The text refers to objects as everything that can be characterized as "this" (*idantayā*).

मय्यखण्डसुखाम्भोधौ बहुधा विश्ववीचय: ।
उत्पद्यन्ते विलीयन्ते मायामारुतविभ्रमात् ॥ ४९६

Due to the whirling winds of māyā, the waves of the universe repeatedly arise and fall in me, the ocean of infinite bliss. (496)

स्थूलादिभावा मयि कल्पिता भ्रमात्
आरोपितानुस्फुरणेन लोकै: ।
काले यथा कल्पकवत्सरायण-
ऋत्वादय: निष्कलनिर्विकल्पे ॥ ४९७

Ideas such as gross (and subtle) are imagined in me by people due to the things superimposed, just as cycles, years, half-years, seasons, etc. are imagined in time, which is indivisible and absolute. (497)

आरोपितं नाश्रयदूषकं भवेत्
कदापि मूढैरतिदोषदूषितै: ।
नाद्रिकरोत्यूषरभूमिभागं
मरीचिका-वारि-महाप्रवाह: ॥ ४९८

That which is superimposed by the profoundly ignorant fools can never affect the substratum. The great flow of water in a mirage does not wet the desert sand. (498)

आकाशवल्लेपविदूरगोऽहं
आदित्यवद्भास्यविलक्षणोऽहम् ।
अहार्यवन्नित्यविनिश्चलोऽहं
अम्भोधिवत्पारविवर्जितोऽहम् ॥ ४९९

Like space, I am beyond contamination. Like the sun, I am different from things illumined. Like the mountain, I am always motionless. Like the ocean, I am boundless. (499)

न मे देहेन सम्बन्धो मेघेनेव विहायस: ।
अत: कुतो मे तद्धर्मा जाग्रत्स्वप्नसुषुप्तय: ॥ ५००

Just as the sky has no connection with the clouds, I have no connection with the body. How then can the states of waking, dream and deep sleep, which belong to it, be mine? (500)

उपाधिरायाति स एव गच्छति
स एव कर्माणि करोति भुङ्क्ते ।
स एव जीर्यन् म्रियते सदाहं
कुलाद्रिवन्निश्चल एव संस्थितः ॥ ५०१

It is limitation which comes and that alone which goes. It alone does work and experiences (the results). It alone ages and dies. I always remain immovable like the Kula mountain. (501)

"Limitation" (*upādhi*)—such as the body and the mind—is what is superimposed on me, the Ātman. All activity, including coming and going, working and experiencing, aging and dying, belongs to the body and mind, not to the Ātman. In Indian mythology, the "Kula mountain" is described as being greatly stable.

न मे प्रवृत्तिर्न च मे निवृत्तिः
सदैकरूपस्य निरंशकस्य ।
एकात्मको यो निबिडो निरन्तरो
व्योमेव पूर्णः स कथं नु चेष्टते ॥ ५०२

There is neither activity nor withdrawal for me, for I am always the same and without parts. How can there be striving in one who is unchanging, compact, without break, and infinite like the space? (502)

Every activity implies change, and requires movable parts and space.

पुण्यानि पापानि निरिन्द्रियस्य
निश्चेतसो निर्विकृतेर्निराकृतेः ।

कुतो ममाखण्डसुखानुभूते:

ब्रूते ह्यनन्वागतमित्यपि श्रुति: ॥ ५०३

How can merit and demerit apply to me, the enjoyer of bliss absolute? For, I am without the senses, without a mind, without a form, and changeless. The Vedas also mention this in the passage, "not touched," etc. (503)

> Merit (*puṇya*) and demerit (*pāpa*) result from the instrumentality of the senses, the mind and the body. I have none of them, hence merit and demerit don't apply to me. The Vedic reference is to the Bṛhadāraṇyaka Upaniṣad (4.3.22).

छायया स्पृष्टमुष्णं वा शीतं वा सुष्ठु दु:ष्ठु वा ।

न स्पृशत्येव यत्किञ्चित्पुरुषं तद्विलक्षणम् ॥ ५०४

Whatever touches a (person's) shadow—heat or cold, good or evil—does not touch the person, who is distinct from it. (504)

> The body is affected by heat or cold. The mind is affected by good or evil. The Ātman is not affected by any of these, because it is different from the body and the mind.

न साक्षिणं साक्ष्यधर्मा: संस्पृशन्ति विलक्षणम् ।

अविकारमुदासीनं गृहधर्मा: प्रदीपवत् ॥ ५०५

The characteristics of what is perceived do not touch the perceiver, who remains distinct, changeless and neutral, just as the characteristics of a home do not touch the lamp (that illumines it). (505)

रवेर्यथा कर्मणि साक्षिभावो
वह्नेर्यथा वाऽयसि दाहकत्वम् ।
रज्जोर्यथाऽऽरोपितवस्तुसङ्ग:
तथैव कूटस्थचिदात्मनो मे ॥ ५०६

As is (1) the sun's being a witness of all activities, (2) the fire's burning power in a piece of iron, and (3) the rope's identity with what is superimposed on it, so is it with the unchanging awareness that I am. (506)

> Like the sun, I am the unattached witness of all activities. The agency of the mind and the senses is projected on me, like the fire's burning power is projected on a piece of (heated) iron. My identity with the body and the mind is fictitious, like the rope's identity with the superimposed snake. In short, I am as unattached as the sun, the fire, and the rope, in the above examples.

कर्तापि वा कारयितापि नाहं
भोक्तापि वा भोजयितापि नाहम् ।
द्रष्टापि वा दर्शयितापि नाहं
सोऽहं स्वयंज्योतिरनीदृगात्मा ॥ ५०७

I neither do nor make others do anything. I neither experience nor make others experience anything. I neither see nor make others see anything. I am the self-effulgent, indescribable being. (507)

चलत्युपाधौ प्रतिबिम्बलौल्यं
औपाधिकं मूढधियो नयन्ति ।
स्वबिम्बभूतं रविवद्विनिष्क्रियं
कर्तास्मि भोक्तास्मि हतोऽस्मि हेति ॥ ५०८

When the limitation (*upādhi*) moves, fools ascribe the movement of the reflection to the object reflected which, like the sun, is free from activity—(and they cry out): "I am the doer," "I am the experiencer," "I am being killed, alas." (508)

> When there is activity in the body and the mind, people mistakenly ascribe it to the Ātman, which is detached and free from any activity. This is like the sun's reflection in water appearing to move due to ripples and waves, and "fools" imagining that it is the sun that is moving.

जले वापि स्थले वापि लुठत्वेष जडात्मक: ।
नाहं विलिप्ये तद्धर्मैर्घटधर्मैर्नभो यथा ॥ ५०९

Let this material body drop down in water or on land. I am not affected by its condition, just as the space (inside a jar) is not affected by the condition of the jar. (509)

कर्तृत्व-भोक्तृत्व-खलत्व-मत्तता-
जडत्व-बद्धत्व-विमुक्तादय: ।
बुद्धेर्विकल्पा न तु सन्ति वस्तुत:
स्वस्मिन्परे ब्रह्मणि केवलेऽद्वये ॥ ५१०

The states of the intellect—such as being a doer or an experiencer, or being cunning, proud, lazy, bound, or free—do not really exist in me, the supreme Brahman, the absolute, the one without a second. (510)

सन्तु विकारा: प्रकृतेर्दशधा शतधा सहस्रधा वापि ।
किं मेऽसङ्गचितस्तैर्न घन: क्वचिदम्बरं स्पृशति ॥ ५११

Let there be tens or hundreds or thousands of ways in which the
material cause (*prakṛti*) is transformed. What have I, the
unattached awareness, got to do with them? Never do the clouds
touch the sky. (511)

अव्यक्तादिस्थूलपर्यन्तमेतत्

विश्वं यत्राभासमात्रं प्रतीतम् ।

व्योमप्रख्यं सूक्ष्ममाद्यन्तहीनं

ब्रह्माद्वैतं यत्तदेवाहमस्मि ॥ ५१२

Brahman, who is nondual, who is like space, subtle, without
beginning or end, and in which this entire universe, from the subtle
to the gross, appears merely as a shadow—that is who I am. (512)

सर्वाधारं सर्ववस्तुप्रकाशं

सर्वाकारं सर्वगं सर्वशून्यम् ।

नित्यं शुद्धं निश्चलं निर्विकल्पं

ब्रह्माद्वैतं यत्तदेवाहमस्मि ॥ ५१३

Brahman, who is nondual and the support of all, who illumines
everything, who has infinite forms, who is all-pervading, who is
devoid of multiplicity, who is eternal, pure, changeless, and absolute
—that is who I am. (513)

यत्प्रत्यस्ताशेषमायाविशेषं

प्रत्यग्रूपं प्रत्ययागम्यमानम् ।

सत्यज्ञानानन्तमानन्दरूपं

ब्रह्माद्वैतं यत्तदेवाहमस्मि ॥ ५१४

Brahman, who is nondual, in whom the endless distinctions of māyā disappear, who is the inmost essence and unknowable, and whose nature is existence, awareness, infinity, and bliss—that is who I am. (514)

> Brahman is the eternal subject, hence it is "unknowable" as an object.

निष्क्रियोऽस्म्यविकारोऽस्मि
निष्कलोऽस्मि निराकृति: ।
निर्विकल्पोऽस्मि नित्योऽस्मि
निरालम्बोऽस्मि निर्द्वय: ॥ ५१५

I am without activity, I am changeless, I am without parts, I am without form, I am absolute, I am eternal, I am without support, and I am nondual. (515)

> I am immutable, hence I am "without parts." I am the support of everything that exists while I am myself "without support," because I need none.

सर्वात्मकोऽहं सर्वोऽहं सर्वातीतोऽहमद्वय: ।
केवलाखण्डबोधोऽहमानन्दोऽहं निरन्तर: ॥ ५१६

I am the self of all, I am all, I transcend all, I am nondual, I am the absolute, I am the infinite awareness, I am bliss, and I am the indivisible. (516)

स्वाराज्यसाम्राज्यविभूतिरेषा
भवत्कृपाश्रीमहिमप्रसादात् ।
प्राप्ता मया श्रीगुरवे महात्मने
नमो नमस्तेऽस्तु पुनर्नमोऽस्तु ॥५१७

I have attained this splendor of sovereignty of self-effulgence through your grace and powerful benediction. Salutations to you, O glorious and great teacher. Salutations to you again and again. (517)

महास्वप्ने मायाकृत-जनि-जरा-मृत्यु-गहने
भ्रमन्तं क्लिश्यन्तं बहुलतर-तापैरनुदिनम् ।
अहंकारव्याघ्र-व्यथितमिममत्यन्तकृपया
प्रबोध्य प्रस्वापात्परमवितवान्मामसि गुरो ॥ ५१८

In the great māyā-generated dream, I was wandering in the forest of birth, decay and death, being tormented day after day by innumerable problems and agitated by the tiger of egoism. O teacher! Through your endless grace you woke me up from my profound sleep and saved me. (518)

नमस्तस्मै सदैकस्मै कस्मैचिन्महसे नमः ।
यदेतद्विश्वरूपेण राजते गुरुराज ते ॥ ५१९

Salutation to you who are always the same. Salutation to you, O king among teachers, whose effulgent awareness shines as this universe. (519)

The Teacher's Response

इति नतमवलोक्य शिष्यवर्यं
समधिगतात्मसुखं प्रबुद्धतत्त्वम् ।
प्रमुदितहृदयं स देशिकेन्द्र:
पुनरिदमाह वच: परं महात्मा ॥ ५२०

Seeing the worthy disciple who had attained the bliss of the self and awakened to the reality with a joyful heart prostrating himself, the noble and great teacher said the following: (520)

ब्रह्मप्रत्ययसंतति-जगदतो ब्रह्मैव तत्सर्वत:
पश्याध्यात्मदृशा प्रशान्तमनसा सर्वास्ववस्थास्वपि ।
रूपादन्यदवेक्षितं किमभितश्चक्षुष्मतां दृश्यते
तद्वद्ब्रह्मविद: सत: किमपरं बुद्धेर्विहारास्पदम् ॥ ५२१

This world is a continuous experience of Brahman, hence it is Brahman in every respect. See it with a serene mind through the lens of the Ātman under all circumstances. Do people with eyes see anything around them other than forms? Likewise, is there anything other than Brahman that is worthy of engaging the minds of the knowers of Brahman? (521)

कस्तां परानन्दरसानुभूतिं
उत्सृज्य शून्येषु रमेत विद्वान् ।
चन्द्रे महाह्लादिनि दीप्यमाने
चित्रेन्दुमालोकयितुं क इच्छेत् ॥ ५२२

What wise person would abandon the experience of supreme bliss
and find pleasure in empty things? When the exceedingly charming
moon is shining, who would want to see a picture of the moon?
(522)

> Things that have a fleeting appearance, with only names and forms
> but no real substance, are "empty."

असत्पदार्थानुभवेन किञ्चित्

न ह्यस्ति तृप्तिर्न च दु:खहानि: ।

तदद्वयानन्दरसानुभूत्या

तृप्त: सुखं तिष्ठ सदात्मनिष्ठया ॥ ५२३

The experience of unreal things provides neither fulfillment nor
removal of sorrow. Being fulfilled through the experience of
nondual bliss, remain happily identified with the real. (523)

स्वमेव सर्वथा पश्यन्मन्यमान: स्वमद्वयम् ।

स्वानन्दमनुभुञ्जान: कालं नय महामते ॥ ५२४

Spend your time, O great one, always perceiving only the self,
looking upon the self as nondual, and enjoying the bliss of the self.
(524)

अखण्डबोधात्मनि निर्विकल्पे

विकल्पनं व्योम्नि पुरप्रकल्पनम् ।

तदद्वयानन्दमयात्मना सदा

शान्तिं परामेत्य भजस्व मौनम् ॥ ५२५

Thinking of the Ātman, the nondual infinite awareness, as diverse is
like imagining a city in the sky. Having attained supreme peace by

constantly identifying with that nondual bliss, you should practice silence. (525)

> To engage with what looks like the external world requires
> identifying with it—which automatically leads to dis-identification
> with the Ātman. To "practice silence" is to keep the focus inward,
> on the Ātman.

तूष्णीमवस्था परमोपशान्ति:
बुद्धेरसत्कल्पविकल्पहेतो: ।
ब्रह्मात्मना ब्रह्मविदो महात्मनो
यत्राद्वयानन्दसुखं निरन्तरम् ॥ ५२६

In the case of a sage who is the knower of Brahman, the mind—
which (in the ignorant) causes the imagination of the unreal—
attains to supreme peace. Identified with Brahman in that state, the
sage enjoys uninterrupted nondual bliss. (526)

नास्ति निर्वासनान्मौनात्परं सुखकृदुत्तमम् ।
विज्ञातात्मस्वरूपस्य स्वानन्दरसपायिन: ॥ ५२७

To one who has experienced one's own nature and enjoyed the bliss
of the Ātman, there is no better source of joy than the silence which
results from being free from desire. (527)

गच्छंस्तिष्ठन्नुपविशञ्छयानो वाऽन्यथापि वा ।
यथेच्छया वसेद्विद्वानात्माराम: सदा मुनि: ॥ ५२८

The enlightened sage, immersed blissfully in the Ātman, remains ever at ease, whether going or staying or sitting or sleeping, or doing anything else. (528)

न देशकालासनदिग्यमादि-
लक्ष्याद्यपेक्षाऽप्रतिबद्धवृत्ते: ।
संसिद्धतत्त्वस्य महात्मनोऽस्ति
स्ववेदने का नियमाद्यवस्था ॥ ५२९

The sage with unobstructed mind who has experienced the truth does not depend on things such as place, time, posture, directions, mental disciplines, and objects of meditation. What rules can there be to know one's own self? (529)

> All "rules" that deal with place (pilgrimage), time (auspicious hours, festival days), posture (for meditation), directions (such as facing the east or the north during worship), mental disciplines (including *yama* and *niyama*, the rules of moral living and moral conduct), and objects of meditation (with or without form and qualities) may help a beginner but, after having "experienced the truth," they are no longer necessary.

घटोऽयमिति विज्ञातुं नियम: कोऽन्ववेक्षते ।
विना प्रमाणसुष्टत्वं यस्मिन्सति पदार्थधी: ॥५३०

Other than a robust means of knowing which provides the knowledge of the object, what rule is needed to know that this is a jar? (530)

अयमात्मा नित्यसिद्ध: प्रमाणे सति भासते ।
न देशं नापि वा कालं न शुद्धिं वाप्यपेक्षते ॥ ५३१

When the means of knowledge are available, this ever-present Ātman is revealed. This does not require a (specific) place or time or purification. (531)

देवदत्तोऽहमित्येतद्विज्ञानं निरपेक्षकम् ।
तद्वद्ब्रह्मविदोऽप्यस्य ब्रह्माहमिति वेदनम् ॥ ५३२

The awareness, "I am Devadatta," is independent of any condition. So is the awareness, "I am Brahman," for the knower of Brahman. (532)

> Devadatta's awareness that "I am Devadatta" does not depend on any external condition. In the same way, the illumined person's awareness that "I am Brahman" does not depend on any external condition.

भानुनेव जगत्सर्वं भासते यस्य तेजसा ।
अनात्मकमसत्तुच्छं किं नु तस्यावभासकम् ॥ ५३३

What indeed can reveal the one whose effulgence, like the sun's, reveals the unreal, worthless and objective universe in its entirety? (533)

> Just as no other light is needed to reveal the sun, no other awareness is needed to reveal Brahman.

वेदशास्त्रपुराणानि भूतानि सकलान्यपि ।
येनार्थवन्ति तं किन्नु विज्ञातारं प्रकाशयेत् ॥ ५३४

What indeed can reveal the knower who makes the Vedas, the Purāṇas, and other scriptures, as well as all beings meaningful? (534)

एष स्वयंज्योतिरनन्तशक्ति:

आत्माऽप्रमेय: सकलानुभूति: ।

यमेव विज्ञाय विमुक्तबन्धो

जयत्ययं ब्रह्मविदुत्तमोत्तम: ॥ ५३५

This Ātman is self-effulgent, infinitely powerful, unknowable (as an object), and experienced by all. Experiencing it and being free from bondage, the supremely eminent knower of Brahman becomes victorious. (535)

> Everyone is aware of their own existence, hence the Ātman as existence (*sat*) is "experienced by all." The conquest of ignorance and its destruction make the knower of Brahman "victorious."

Freedom from Bondage

न खिद्यते नो विषयै: प्रमोदते

न सज्जते नापि विरज्यते च ।

स्वस्मिन्सदा क्रीडति नन्दति स्वयं

निरन्तरानन्दरसेन तृप्त: ॥ ५३६

Filled with unceasing bliss, the knower of Brahman sports and delights in the Ātman, neither grieved nor overjoyed by sense objects, and neither attached to nor detached from them. (536)

क्षुधां देहव्यथां त्यक्त्वा बाल: क्रीडति वस्तुनि ।

तथैव विद्वान् रमते निर्ममो निरहं सुखी ॥ ५३७

Disregarding the pain of hunger, a child plays with toys. The enlightened being delights in the same way, blissful and free from the sense of "I" and "mine." (537)

चिन्ताशून्यमदैन्यभैक्षमशनं पानं सरिद्वारिषु
स्वातन्त्र्येण निरंकुशा स्थितिरभीर्निन्द्रा शमशाने वने ।
वस्त्रं क्षालन-शोषणादि-रहितं दिग्वास्तु शय्या मही
संचारो निगमान्तवीथिषु विदां क्रीडा परे ब्रह्मणि ॥ ५३८

The enlightened being sports in the supreme Brahman while living on alms without anxiety or humiliation, drinking the water of a river, living independently with freedom, sleeping fearlessly in a cremation ground or a forest, wearing perhaps nothing, which needs no washing and drying, sleeping on the ground, and wandering on the paths of Vedānta. (538)

> The text's version of "wearing nothing" is a typical usage in Sanskrit: "having four directions—east, west, north and south—as the only cloth" (*dig-vastra* or *dig-ambara*).

विमानमालम्ब्य शरीरमेतत्
भुनक्त्यशेषान्विषयानुपस्थितान् ।
परेच्छया बालवदात्मवेत्ता
योऽव्यक्तलिङ्गोऽननुषक्तबाह्य: ॥ ५३९

Unattached to the externals and with no outward mark, the knower of the Ātman experiences, like a child, the innumerable sense objects as they present themselves through others' wish, without identifying with the body. (539)

> Illumined beings are difficult to recognize because they have "no outward mark." They experience the world "like a child," without any prejudice or bias. They don't initiate any activity prompted by their own wishes, but merely experience what appears before them.

दिगम्बरो वापि च साम्बरो वा

त्वगम्बरो वापि चिदम्बरस्थ: ।

उन्मत्तवद्वापि च बालवद्वा

पिशाचवद्वापि चरत्यवन्याम् ॥ ५४०

Established in the state of awareness, the knower of the Ātman may wander in the world like a mad person, or like a child, or like a ghoul, wearing clothes or skins or wearing nothing at all. (540)

> The knower of the Ātman is beyond any stereotypes. This reiterates what the previous verse states, that they have no identifiable "outward mark."

कामान्निष्कामरुपी संश्चरत्येकचरो मुनि: ।

स्वात्मनैव सदा तुष्ट: स्वयं सर्वात्मना स्थित: ॥ ५४१

The sage moves alone among sense objects, free from desires, remaining ever content in the Ātman, and dwelling as the self of all. (541)

> Dwelling "as the self of all," the knower of the Ātman sees everyone in the Ātman, and sees the Ātman in everyone.

क्वचिन्मूढो विद्वान् क्वचिदपि महाराजविभव:
क्वचिद्भ्रान्त: सौम्य: क्वचिदजगराचारकलित: ।
क्वचित्पात्रीभूत: क्वचिदवमत: क्वाप्यविदित:
चरत्येवं प्राज्ञ: सततपरमानन्दसुखिन: ॥ ५४२

Enjoying abiding supreme bliss, the knower (of the Ātman) lives
sometimes as a fool, sometimes as a scholar, sometimes as a
powerful emperor, sometimes confused, sometimes gentle,
sometimes like an unmoving python, sometimes honored,
sometimes disrespected, and sometimes even unknown. (542)

> The illumined being is viewed by others in diverse ways but
> remains supremely unconcerned about it. Just as "an unmoving
> python" waits for the food to come to it, the illumined being does
> not initiate any activity but merely remains witness to everything.

निर्धनोऽपि सदा तुष्टोऽप्यसहायो महाबल: ।
नित्यतृप्तोऽप्यभुञ्जानोऽप्यसम: समदर्शन: ॥ ५४३

(The knower of the Ātman) may be (1) without wealth and yet ever
content, (2) without help and yet very powerful, (3) without food
and yet always satisfied, and (4) without equal and yet seeing
everyone as equals. (543)

> The "food" includes not only what the body consumes but also
> what is taken in by the mind and the senses.

अपि कुर्वन्नकुर्वाणश्चाभोक्ता फलभोग्यपि ।
शरीर्यप्यशरीर्येष परिच्छिन्नोऽपि सर्वग: ॥ ५४४

(The knower of the Ātman) works and yet is inactive, experiences the results of karma and yet remains unaffected, possesses a body and yet is not identified with it, is limited and yet all-pervading. (544)

अशरीरं सदा सन्तमिमं ब्रह्मविदं क्वचित् ।
प्रियाप्रिये न स्पृशतस्तथैव च शुभाशुभे ॥ ५४५

Neither pleasant nor unpleasant, neither good nor evil ever touches the knower of Brahman, who lives without identifying with the body. (545)

See the Chāndogya Upaniṣad (8.12.1).

स्थूलादिसम्बन्धवतोऽभिमानिनः
सुखं च दुःखं च शुभाशुभे च ।
विध्वस्तबन्धस्य सदात्मनो मुनेः
कुतः शुभं वाऽप्यशुभं फलं वा ॥ ५४६

Happiness and sorrow, good and evil, affect one who is attached to the gross body etc., and identifies with them. How can good or even evil, or its result, affect the sage who identifies with the real and has destroyed bondage? (546)

The "etc." includes both the subtle body (the mind, the intellect, the ego) as well as the sense objects.

तमसा ग्रस्तवद्भानादग्रस्तोऽपि रविर्जनैः ।
ग्रस्त इत्युच्यते भ्रान्त्या ह्यज्ञात्वा वस्तुलक्षणम् ॥ ५४७

Being unaware of the sun's true nature, people are deluded into speaking of it as having been swallowed when it appears be swallowed but is not really swallowed. (547)

> In Indian mythology, the solar eclipse is described as the swallowing of the sun by Rāhu. It is delusion to think that "the sun's true nature"—light—can be extinguished.

तद्वद्देहादिबन्धेभ्यो विमुक्तं ब्रह्मवित्तमम् ।
पश्यन्ति देहिवन्मूढा: शरीराभासदर्शनात् ॥ ५४८

In the same way, fools think of the perfect knower of Brahman, who is free from the bondage of body etc., as possessing a body, seeing only an appearance of it. (548)

> The knower of Brahman is free from the bondage of not only the body but also the mind and the senses.

अहिनिर्ल्वयनीवायं मुक्तदेहस्तु तिष्ठति ।
इतस्ततश्चाल्यमानो यत्किञ्चित्प्राणवायुना ॥ ५४९

Just as the skin of a snake moves slightly here and there by the wind, so is the body of the liberated one by prāṇa. (549)

स्रोतसा नीयते दारु यथा निम्नोन्नतस्थलम् ।
दैवेन नीयते देहो यथाकालोपभुक्तिषु ॥ ५५०

Just as a water current tosses a log of wood up and down, so does nature carry the body to experience its karma results whenever they are due. (550)

प्रारब्धकर्म-परिकल्पित-वासनाभि:
संसारिवच्चरति भुक्तिषु मुक्तदेह: ।
सिद्ध: स्वयं वसति साक्षिवदत्र तूष्णीं
चक्रस्य मूलमिव कल्पविकल्प-शून्य: ॥ ५५१

Free from (identification with) the body, the jīvanmukta moves among sense objects like a worldly person through desires generated by prārabdha karma, staying silent like a witness, and without movement like the hub of a wheel. (551)

> The jīvanmukta is "without movement" of the mind, meaning, there is no identification with the turbulent thought currents that continually weigh pros and cons.

नैवेन्द्रियाणि विषयेषु नियुंक्त एष
नैवापयुंक्त उपदर्शन-लक्षणस्थ: ।
नैव क्रियाफलमपीषदवेक्षते स
स्वानन्द-सान्द्र-रसपान-सुमत्तचित्त: ॥ ५५२

With the mind fully absorbed (in the Ātman) by drinking the bliss of the Ātman, the jīvanmukta neither attaches the senses to their objects nor detaches them from these but remains a witness, without caring in the least for even the results of karma. (552)

लक्ष्यालक्ष्यगतिं त्यक्त्वा यस्तिष्ठेत्केवलात्मना ।
शिव एव स्वयं साक्षादयं ब्रह्मविदुत्तम: ॥ ५५३

Abandoning all concern about what the goal is or isn't, one who dwells as the absolute Ātman is verily Śiva and is the best among the knowers of Brahman. (553)

> One who is identified with the Ātman no longer needs to think of "the goal." Śiva is the embodiment of auspiciousness.

जीवन्नेव सदा मुक्त: कृतार्थो ब्रह्मवित्तम: ।
उपाधिनाशाद्ब्रह्मैव सन् ब्रह्माप्येति निर्द्वयम् ॥ ५५४

With the destruction of all limitations, the supreme knower of Brahman becomes ever-free even while living, realizing life's purpose and, being Brahman all along, attains the nondual Brahman. (554)

> See the Bṛhadāraṇyaka Upaniṣad (4.4.6). When one's identity as Brahman is experienced, it *feels* as if one "attains" it, even though that is what one has been "all along."

शैलूषो वेषसद्भावाभावयोश्च यथा पुमान् ।
तथैव ब्रह्मविच्छ्रेष्ठ: सदा ब्रह्मैव नापर: ॥ ५५५

The actor remains a man, whether or not he is in costume. In the same way, the supreme knower of Brahman is always Brahman, never anyone else. (555)

यत्र क्वापि विशीर्ण सत्पर्णमिव तरोर्वपु: पततात् ।
ब्रह्मीभूतस्य यते: प्रागेव तच्चिदग्निना दग्धम् ॥ ५५६

Let the body of the sage who is identified with Brahman wither and fall anywhere like the dried leaf of a tree. It has already been burnt in the fire of knowledge. (556)

The "fire of knowledge" is the awareness of being Brahman, not the body. Hence where and how the body dies is of no consequence.

सदात्मनि ब्रह्मणि तिष्ठतो मुने:

पूर्णाद्वियानन्दमयात्मना सदा ।

न देशकालाद्युचितप्रतीक्षा

त्वङ्-मांस-विट्-पिण्डविसर्जनाय ॥ ५५७

For the sage always identified with Brahman, the real and infinite nondual bliss, there is no need to wait for the appropriate place, time etc., in order to discard this mass of skin, flesh and filth. (557)

देहस्य मोक्षो नो मोक्षो न दण्डस्य कमण्डलो: ।

अविद्याहृदयग्रन्थिमोक्षो मोक्षो यतस्तत: ॥ ५५८

Freedom from the body (through death) is not freedom, neither is it the freedom of (giving up) the staff or the water bowl, because (real) freedom is the freedom from the knot of ignorance in the heart. (558)

Mere outward renunciation of the insignia of monastic life, the staff and the water bowl, do not indicate freedom. The source of bondage is in the mind, not in material things. The "knot of ignorance in the heart" is the seeming identification of the Ātman with the body and the mind.

कुल्यायामथ नद्यां वा शिवक्षेत्रेऽपि चत्वरे ।

पर्णं पतति चेत्तेन तरो: किं नु शुभाशुभम् ॥ ५५९

If a leaf falls in a stream or a river or a place dedicated to Śiva or at an intersection, does it matter to a tree if that is auspicious or not? (559)

पत्रस्य पुष्पस्य फलस्य नाशवद्
देहेन्द्रियप्राणधियां विनाश: ।
नैवात्मन: स्वस्य सदात्मकस्य
आनन्दाकृतेर्वृक्षवदस्ति चैष: ॥ ५६०

The destruction of the body, the senses, the prāṇa, and the mind is like the destruction of a leaf or a flower or a fruit. It does not mean the destruction of one's own real self, the Ātman, the embodiment of bliss, which survives like the tree. (560)

> The tree survives the destruction of its leaves, flowers and fruits. In the same way, the Ātman survives the destruction of the body, the mind, the senses, and the prāṇa.

प्रज्ञानघन इत्यात्मलक्षणं सत्यसूचकम् ।
अनूद्यौपाधिकस्यैव कथयन्ति विनाशनम् ॥ ५६१

Describing the characteristic of the Ātman as pure awareness, which indicates that it is real, the Vedas describe the destruction of only the limitations. (561)

> See the Bṛhadāraṇyaka Upaniṣad (4.5.13). The destruction of the body, the senses, the prāṇa, and the mind (#560) is the destruction of what *appears* to be real but really is not. All of those are ignorance-induced "limitations" (*upādhi*) on the Ātman, which is the only reality.

अविनाशी वा अरेऽयमात्मेति श्रुतिरात्मन: ।
प्रब्रवीत्यविनाशित्वं विनश्यत्सु विकारिषु ॥ ५६२

"This Ātman is indeed indestructible," say the Vedas, declaring the Ātman's indestructibility in the midst of things that change and are destructible. (562)

The quoted passage is from the Bṛhadāraṇyaka Upaniṣad (4.5.14).

पाषाण-वृक्ष-तृण-धान्य-कटाम्बराद्या:
दग्धा भवन्ति हि मृदेव यथा तथैव ।
देहेन्द्रियासुमन-आदि-समस्तदृश्यं
ज्ञानाग्निदग्धमुपयाति परात्मभावम् ॥ ५६३

Just as a stone, a tree, the grass, the grain, the straw, and the cloth become nothing but earth (ashes) when burnt, so do the body, the senses, the prāṇa, the mind, etc., become the supreme Ātman when burnt in the fire of knowledge. (563)

विलक्षणं यथा ध्वान्तं लीयते भानुतेजसि ।
तथैव सकलं दृश्यं ब्रह्मणि प्रविलीयते ॥ ५६४

Darkness, which is distinct (from sunshine), vanishes in the radiance of the sun. In the same way, the entire universe dissolves in Brahman. (564)

घटे नष्टे यथा व्योम व्योमैव भवति स्फुटम् ।
तथैवोपाधिविलये ब्रह्मैव ब्रह्मवित्स्वयम् ॥ ५६५

When a jar is broken, the space enclosed in it becomes obvious as (the limitless) space. In the same way, when the limitations dissolve, the knower of Brahman becomes Brahman itself. (565)

क्षीरं क्षीरे यथा क्षिप्तं तैलं तैले जलं जले ।
संयुक्तमेकतां याति तथाऽऽत्मन्यात्मविन्मुनि: ॥ ५६६

Milk poured into milk, or oil into oil, or water into water, becomes united and one with it. In the same way, the sage who has experienced the Ātman becomes one with the Ātman. (566)

एवं विदेहकैवल्यं सन्मात्रत्वमखण्डितम् ।
ब्रह्मभावं प्रपद्यैष यतिर्नावर्तते पुन: ॥ ५६७

In this way, attaining liberation after death and eternal oneness with Brahman the absolute reality, this sage is not born again. (567)

Even the seeming identification with the body in the jīvanmukta state ends with death and there is no returning to this false world created by ignorance.

सदात्मैकत्वविज्ञानदग्धाविद्यादिवष्र्मण: ।
अमुष्य ब्रह्मभूतत्वाद् ब्रह्मण: कुत उद्भव: ॥ ५६८

When the body of ignorance, etc. is burnt by the experience of oneness of the embodied self and Brahman, the sage becomes Brahman. How can Brahman have birth (again)? (568)

The "body of ignorance etc." includes both the cause (ignorance) and also the effects—the "three bodies" (gross, subtle, causal)

(#72-123) or the "five layers" (#149-209). All these effects vanish when the cause is "burnt" by the "fire" of knowledge.

मायाक्लृप्तौ बन्धमोक्षौ न स्तः स्वात्मनि वस्तुतः ।
यथा रज्जौ निष्क्रियायां सर्पाभासविनिर्गमौ ॥ ५६९

Like the appearance and disappearance of the snake in an unmoving rope, both bondage and liberation are conjured up by māyā and do not really exist in the Ātman. (569)

आवृतेः सदसत्त्वाभ्यां वक्तव्ये बन्धमोक्षणे ।
नावृतिर्ब्रह्मणः काचिदन्याभावादनावृतम् ।
यद्यस्त्यद्वैतहानिः स्याद् द्वैतं नो सहते श्रुतिः ॥ ५७०

Bondage or liberation may be spoken of when there is presence or absence of the veil. But there is nothing to veil Brahman, who remains uncovered in the absence of anything else. Should anything else exist, nonduality would become untenable. The Vedas don't support duality. (570)

The "veil" is provided by the veiling power of ignorance. The rejection of duality can be found in, for instance, the Chāndogya Upaniṣad (6.2.1) and the Kaṭha Upaniṣad (4.11).

बन्धश्च मोक्षश्च मृषैव मूढा
बुद्धेर्गुणं वस्तुनि कल्पयन्ति ।
दृगावृतिं मेघकृतां यथा रवौ
यतोऽद्वयासङ्गचिदेतदक्षरम् ॥ ५७१

Bondage and liberation are both false. The attributes of the mind are imagined to be attributes of the Ātman, just as the veiling of the eyes by the clouds is imagined to be the veiling of the sun (by the clouds). For, the imperishable Ātman is nondual, unattached awareness. (571)

> The idea of bondage and liberation belong to the mind, not to the Ātman. "The mind alone is the cause of both bondage and liberation" (Amṛtabindu Upaniṣad, 2).

अस्तीति प्रत्ययो यश्च यश्च नास्तीति वस्तुनि ।
बुद्धेरेव गुणावेतौ न तु नित्यस्य वस्तुनः ॥ ५७२

Both these ideas—that the bondage exists in the Ātman and that it does not—belong to the mind, and not to the eternal Ātman. (572)

> (1) The Ātman is bound due to ignorance and (2) it is subsequently liberated through knowledge—both these ideas are the mind's creations. The eternally free Ātman is never bound, hence has no need to be liberated.

अतस्तौ मायया क्लृप्तौ बन्धमोक्षौ न चात्मनि ।
निष्कले निष्क्रिये शान्ते निरवद्ये निरञ्जने ।
अद्वितीये परे तत्त्वे व्योमवत्कल्पना कुतः ॥ ५७३

Hence bondage and liberation conjured up by māyā do not exist in the Ātman. How can these be imagined in the supreme reality which is (infinite) like space, undivided, without activity, calm, without defects, and taintless? (573)

न निरोधो न चोत्पत्तिर्न बद्धो न च साधक: ।

न मुमुक्षुर्न वै मुक्त इत्येषा परमार्थता ॥ ५७४

This is the highest truth—there is no death, no birth, no one bound, no one striving, no seeker of liberation, and no one liberated. (574)

> This verse occurs in both the Amṛtabindu Upaniṣad (10) and in the Māṇḍukya Kārikā (2. 32).

सकल-निगम-चूडा-स्वान्त-सिद्धान्तरूपं

परमिदमतिगुह्यं दर्शितं ते मयाद्य ।

अपगत-कलिदोषं काम-निर्मुक्त-बुद्धिं

स्वसुतवदसकृत्त्वां भावयित्वा मुमुक्षुम् ॥ ५७५

This inmost truth regarding the self, which is the supreme and profound secret at the pinnacle of all Vedic wisdom, is today repeatedly revealed by me to you, as I would to my own son, because I think of you as one who (1) longs for liberation, (2) is free from the defects of kali yuga, and (3) has a mind free from desires. (575)

> The "defects of kali yuga" are the material propensities of the present era (yuga), which is the lowest in the cyclical order of four eras: Satya, Tretā, Dvāpara, Kali.

इति श्रुत्वा गुरोर्वाक्यं प्रश्रयेण कृतानति: ।

स तेन समनुज्ञातो ययौ निर्मुक्तबन्धन: ॥ ५७६

Hearing these words of the teacher, the disciple prostrated before him with reverence and, with his permission, went away liberated from bondage. (576)

गुरुरेष सदानन्दसिन्धौ निर्मग्नमानस: ।
पावयन्वसुधां सर्वां विचचार निरन्तर: ॥ ५७७

Blessing the entire world, the teacher continued to wander, with the mind deeply immersed in the blissful ocean of existence. (577)

इत्याचार्यस्य शिष्यस्य संवादेनात्मलक्षणम् ।
निरूपितं मुमुक्षूणां सुखबोधोपपत्तये ॥ ५७८

In this way, through the conversation between the teacher and the disciple, the nature of the Ātman has been taught for an easy understanding of those longing for liberation. (578)

हितमिदमुपदेशमाद्रियन्तां
विहित-निरस्त-समस्त-चित्तदोषा: ।
भवसुख-विरता: प्रशान्त-चित्ता:
श्रुति-रसिका यतयो मुमुक्षवो ये ॥ ५७९

May this beneficial teaching be appreciated by those seekers who (1) have removed all the defects of the mind, (2) are detached from worldly enjoyments, (3) have minds that are supremely calm, (4) find joy in the Vedas, and (5) long for liberation. (579)

संसाराध्वनि ताप-भानुकिरण-प्रोद्भूत-दाह-व्यथा-
खिन्नानां जलकांक्षया मरुभुवि भ्रान्त्या परिभ्राम्यताम् ।
अत्यासन्न-सुधाम्बुधिं सुखकरं ब्रह्माद्वयं दर्शयति
एषा शङ्करभारती विजयते निर्वाण-संदायिनी ॥ ५८०

Those who are scorched on the paths of saṁsāra by the burning pain caused by the heat of the sun's rays and through delusion roam around searching for water in desert sands—to them this glorious and hopeful message shows the ocean of nectar which is extremely near, the blissful, nondual Brahman, and leads them to liberation. (580)

> The deluded who suffer in this saṁsāra run after every mirage in the desert in search of water. This text shows them that their pain and thirst can vanish from a source that is closest to them—their own true self, which is "the blissful, nondual Brahman."

※

Glossary

Ātman (lit., self) is the real me, who is birthless and deathless, pure and perfect. The real me remains covered, as it were, by what are conceived as three bodies (*śarīra*): gross (*sthūla*), subtle (*sūkṣma*), and causal (*kāraṇa*). The coverings are, alternatively, also viewed as five layers (*kośa*), namely, layers of food (*annamaya*), of prāṇa (*prāṇamaya*), of the mind (*manomaya*), of knowledge (*vijñānamaya*), and of bliss (*ānandamaya*). Ātman and Brahman refer to the same reality. When the reality is spoken of in relation to an individual, it is called Ātman; in relation to everyone and everything, the reality is known as Brahman.

Brahman (lit., vast, infinite) is the one who is real. Anything other than Brahman is only a fleeting appearance (*mithyā*), not real. Although beyond the reach of the mind and the senses, and hence indescribable, Brahman is nevertheless described as absolute existence (*sat*), consciousness (*cit*) and infinity (*ananta*). What this really means is that Brahman is *not* nonexistent, *not* material, and *not* finite. Brahman is beyond all categorization and ideation.

Guṇa (lit., attribute, rope) is māyā's attribute. There are three *guṇas*: *tamas* (representing dullness or inertia), *rajas* (representing restlessness or activity) and *sattva* (representing harmony or purity). These three strands form the "rope" of māyā, which seemingly binds the Ātman to the material world.

Indriya (senses) are the subtle counterparts of the tangible organs. There are five senses of knowledge (*jñānendriya*)—ears, skin, eyes, nose, and tongue—which help us experience five kinds of sense objects (*viṣaya*): sound, touch, sight, smell, and taste. There are five senses of action (*karmendriya*)—speech, hands, feet, and organs of excretion and procreation—which control speech, manual activity, locomotion, excretion, and reproduction. It is important to distinguish the senses from the organs: the organs are parts of the gross body; the senses belong to the subtle body and therefore survive physical death. The sense of hearing, for instance, is not the ear per se, but the *ability* to hear, which is accomplished through the instrumentality of ears.

Jīva is Brahman who has apparently become individualized through ignorance and identified with a body/mind as "I" (*aham*) or "mine" (*mama*).

Jīvanmukta is one who is spiritually free (*mukta*) even while living (*jīvan*). In order to go to heaven, it is necessary to die, but the experience of one's identity as Ātman or Brahman can be had here and now. After knowing that "I am Brahman" (*ahaṁ brahmāsmi*) and abiding in that experience, the person continues to live in freedom (*jīvanmukti*). When the body eventually dies, there is no rebirth and the enlightened one attains to the freedom beyond the body (*videhamukti*).

Karma (lit., work) is activity, physical or mental, which results in (1) the experience of joy (*sukha*) or sorrow (*duḥkha*) and (2) subtle mental impressions (*saṁskāra*) which may influence (but never determine) future activity. The sum total of *saṁskāras* at any given time is the measure of a person's character. The effects of karma (*karma-phala*) are inexorable, but the composition of *saṁskāras* can be changed by consciously changing one's thoughts and actions.

Pañcikaraṇa is the process through which the five (*pañca*) subtle primary elements (*tanmātrā*)—the essence of space, air, fire, water, and earth—combine to become five tangible elements (*mahābhūta*) —which, in turn, combine to form the material universe (*jagat*).

Prāṇa is the life-force that animates the body and the mind, making both voluntary and involuntary activities possible, such as breathing, yawning, sneezing, secreting, and leaving the body upon death. Depending on its major functions, it has five subdivisions known as *prāṇa, apāna, vyāna, udāna,* and *samāna.* It is a part of what is conceived as the subtle body.

Samādhi is the state of immersion or absorption. When distinctions (*vikalpa*) persist even in the absorbed state, it is called a differentiated (*savikalpa,* lit. "with distinctions") samādhi. When all distinctions disappear in a completely nondual experience, it is called an undifferentiated (*nirvikalpa,* lit. "without distinctions") samādhi.

Saṁsāra is the world of appearances, fleeting and continually changing. Because it is something in which we are hopelessly enmeshed, it is often compared to the ocean (*sāgara*) which is difficult to cross. Because it keeps us in a vicious loop created by karma and its effects, leading from one birth to the next, it is also compared to a circle (*cakra*), which has no beginning and no end. The only way to demolish the circular path once and for all is through a conscious and vigorous effort to attain freedom (*mokṣa*).

Vedānta (lit., the essence of the Vedas) is the Vedic wisdom that undergirds and inspires the various traditions in Hinduism. In a secondary sense, Vedanta means the Upaniṣads, the philosophical portion (*jñānakāṇḍa*) of the Vedas. Derived from the Sanskrit root *vid* ("to know"), Vedanta can also be understood as "the essence of knowledge." In that sense, it may stand for the perennial wisdom derived from the spiritual revelations in different religious traditions throughout history.

Vṛtti is a form the mind takes when it comes in contact with objects, the way water takes the form of the container it occupies. If the mind is imagined to be a lake, a *vṛtti* is a "wave" produced by every perception, thought, feeling, and memory. Stilling of these waves, according to Patañjali, leads to concentration (*yoga*).

✳

Index

Numbers indicate verses, not pages.

Also by Swami Tyagananda

Walking the Walk: A Karma Yoga Manual

Knowing the Knower: A Jnana Yoga Manual

Amṛtabindu Upaniṣad

Insights from the Gita (Audio)

Kathopanishad (Audio)

Narada Bhakti Sutra (Audio)

www.ingramcontent.com/pod-product-compliance
Lightning Source LLC
LaVergne TN
LVHW051502080426
835509LV00017B/1887